MW00559575

You Already Know.

A Playwright's Guide to Trusting Yourself.
Practical Exercises to Open the Channel.

Aaron Henne

writ large press
los angeles

Writ Large Press
Los Angeles, CA
www.writlargepress.com
www.aaronhenne.com

Cover Image by Judeth Oden
Book layout by Judeth Oden
Author photo by MaryBeth Bentwood

I dream, therefore I exist.
August Strindberg, *The Madman's Defense*

A book is like a child: it is easier to bring it into the world
than to control it when it is launched there.
George Bernard Shaw

FOR JULIE

FOREWORD
[by al watt]

People have all sorts of opinions when it comes to the creative process. "You've either got talent or you don't." We hear this all the time; the implication being that only those who show obvious ability straight out of the gate ought to pursue their calling, while everyone else should just stay home. It also suggests that if one does not display immediate signs that they could be "the best," then they best not bother.

As one examines this line of reasoning, it very quickly begins to fall apart. One need not look far to cite myriad examples of "greatness" that sprang from such humble beginnings. One could hardly imagine that the community was falling over themselves to drive these paragons of mediocrity to practice. We have heard countless stories, from Michael Jordan not making the varsity squad to Einstein failing math. Quentin Tarantino's first film was called *The Birthday Party*. Ever seen it? Me neither. Steve Prefontaine was told that his legs were too short to be a great runner. The realm of genius is littered with runts whose hearts were bigger than the noble minds who wished to tame them.

If you ever go to a book signing and they have that question and answer thing at the end, ask the writer if the first novel he wrote got published. How about the second, or the third? Ask how many words he wrote before he finally did get published.

People speak of talent as though it were simply a happy genetic accident or some quantifiable resource. I believe talent is the absence of something. I believe it is the absence of limiting thoughts around an activity. In the absence of limits, one's focus shifts. There is no definable result to measure one's self against, and one relaxes into the activity, more consumed with exploration than result.

What I'm trying to say is that I believe talent is joy.

It is the embracing of an activity with such desire and obsession that it becomes the dream-scape of one's existence. What some call talent may simply be a love affair with the gods of one's desire.

When we remember that we are simply channels for the story that wants to be told through us, we become curious and the thrill of creation becomes its own reward. When one humbles one's self on the page, disparate thoughts begin to organize, and words are revealed that oftentimes astonish their creator.

Dylan Thomas writes of "the force that through the green fuse drives the flower." Is it possible that perhaps the flower is simply our joy and curiosity on the page?

This brings me to Aaron Henne's very excellent book of writing exercises. Aaron understands that writing can't be taught. It can't, because it isn't supposed to be. The writer, by definition, toils alone on the outer fringe, suspicious of rules and despising convention. Writers are seekers.

When Aaron asked me to write the foreword, I didn't know what he was sending me, but when I started reading the exercises, I could feel my imagination heating up. After twenty minutes, I put the book down and started using the exercise on page 31. Almost immediately I cracked a story problem that I had been struggling with for a while. I continued reading, and then stopped again in the middle 50s to try another one. It was late, and I never write at night (not since I got married), but this was good. I didn't get a lot of sleep that night, but I made some progress.

What Aaron has created with this book is the antidote to writer's block, a mother lode of writing exercises designed to shake things up. These exercises give us permission to get out of our left-brain, and tap into our joy, the seat of our genius. As far as I'm concerned, this is the most effective way to get the story from the imagination onto the page.

Artists don't need teachers, at least not in the traditional sense. We need an environment that engages our imagination and allows us to explore the world of our story. What Aaron has assembled here is an invaluable tool for all writers, novice to pro. A comprehensive series of exercises that ignite the imagination and speak directly to the basic tension that lies at the heart of every story. It's a fun, user-friendly tool to aid the writer in finding the story that dwells within. Use it.

—Al Watt (author of the novel *Diamond Dogs*, founder
and creative director of LA Writers Lab)

TABLE OF CONTENTS

INTRODUCTION

Creating a Draft   2.
How to Use this Book   3.

THE BEGINNING

On (Not) Figuring It Out   9.
Loosen Up   10.
The Character Creation Visualization   11.
Gates of Heaven   13.
The Space Visualization   14.
The First Scene   15.
The First Dialogue   16.
News of the Day   18.
Essences   20.
Scene Composition   21.
Dream a Little Dream   23.
On Structure   24.
Myth Making   25.
Rewriting the Myth   26.
Borrowing from the Masters   27.
Lost Objects   29.
On Stamina   31.
The Seven Meritorious Practices Play   32.
On Tactics   36.
Tactical Uses   37.
Musical...the Musical!   38.
Verse and Prose   39.
The Child Inside   40.

15 Minutes to Live   41.
Forget the Past   42.
Facing Fears   43.
The Stages of Grief   44.
Inanimate Relations   47.
Inanimate Intimacy   48.
Pedestrian/Abstract   49.
Say It, Do It, Live It   50.
Say it Ain't So   51.
          On Research   52.
The Power of the Group   54.
Group Exercises   55.
          Be Here Now   57.

THE MIDDLE

          On Clarity   61.
The Letter   62.
The Monologue   63.
The Conversation   64.
Prologue   65.
The Last Scene   66.
The Last Last Scene   67.
Collage   68.
And God Talks Back   70.
Opposing Words   72.
Don't Go There   73.
          On Motifs   74.
Rewriting Your Myth   75.
Grief Never Dies   76.
Breathe   78.
Sympathy for the Devil   79.
Climaxing   81.
Make Me Laugh   82.
Make Me Laugh Again   83.
Playing with Music   84.
Found Objects   85.
Four Monologues, Two Scenes
and So Much More   88.

Dream a Bigger Dream   90.
Say Say Say   91.
Epilogue   92.
       Be Here Now   93.

THE END

       On Putting it Together   97.
Operating Metaphor   98.
Mind the Gap   99.
10 Minute, 20 Minute,
30 Minute...Draft!   100.
Filling it in   102.
Congratulations   103.
Read!!   104.
This is Critical   106.
       Be Here Now   107.

THE BEGINNING

       On "Rewriting"   111.
There is No One Way   112.
Attention Must Be Paid!   113.
No Ifs, Ands, or Buts   114.
The New Play   115.
Magnification   116.
This One's My Favorite   117.
They Are All My Favorites   118.
       On Knowing   119.
       Be Here Now   120.

THE MIDDLE

       On Waiting   125.
Giving it Away   126.
Readings and Staged Readings
and Workshops...Oh My!   127.
       Be Here Now   129.

THE END

Out in the World   133.

Who Do You Like?   134.

Submission   135.

On Humility   136.

On Confidence   137.

Be Here Now   138.

THE BEGINNING

INTRODUCTION

We begin.
We are in the middle.
We end.

We begin again.

CREATING A DRAFT

Here's how I usually write a play:
About twenty different notions, characters and scenarios enter my consciousness.
They come from everywhere—dreams, news stories, poems, novels, family histories and friends' suggestions.
I beg, borrow and steal.
I have no shame.
Three or four of these ideas stick with me.
I start writing, exploring, dreaming on the page.
I try putting this character in that situation.
I write speeches.
I write single lines that I know belong in someone's mouth.
I write people trying to escape or trying to stay put.
I ask questions.
I find out that I need more information.
I research.
I write some more.
One of the stories starts to take the lead.
I know it is doing so because I can't stop thinking about the characters and their desires.
Their needs thrill, sadden and scare me.
I write some more.
Eventually, a critical mass is reached.
I put the pieces together.
I read.
I see that connections have been missed.
I fill in the gaps.
I read.
I hear that the story has just begun.
I write some more.
I read.
I feel that a moment over here needs to be set up more effectively over there.
I fill in the gaps.
I read.
I see, hear and feel the play.
I write some more.
I have a draft.

Then, I write some more.

HOW TO USE THIS BOOK

You may follow this book from beginning to end, using it as a road-map towards the creation of a full length play.

THE BEGINNING is made up of channel opening exercises meant to expose character and give you an array of writing techniques. You will discover that connections can be made through seemingly disconnected elements. You will write by using inspirations from the world around you. Every scene will not be golden and every monologue won't result in a rush of important realizations. Every page, however, will have something to share about your developing play. A character may tell you the secret of life and even if he winds up left out of your "final" piece, what he has to say is important. Or a solitary stage direction may reveal where your play starts.

Here, at the beginning, you may not yet see these landmarks, pointing you towards your play. They are, however, there, waiting for you to recognize them.

After writing your heart out in the first section, you will read through your writings and find the characters who interest you, the plot points that intrigue and the themes which call through the night. In THE MIDDLE you will focus on producing a number of scenes, dialogues, mimes and moments which augment and explore more deeply the elements you discovered in THE BEGINNING.

When you reach THE END, you will look at the mountains of produced work to find your play. You will be pleasantly surprised by moments you forgot you wrote and scenes which take on different meanings than you initially intended. You will create a first draft by putting these elements together, thus discovering that you, in fact, knew exactly what you were doing.

Then, you start anew.
Kind of.

In THE BEGINNING (Part Deux) you will look honestly at the work and find even more exciting ways to get curious and go deeper. AKA Rewriting.

Finally, the last sections (THE MIDDLE, THE END...) deal with the nature of trusting your-self through the challenges and excitement of getting the work on its feet.
Production.

Begin.
OR
Take the book with you.
To the beach.
To the park.

To the office.
Open a page at random.
Do an exercise.
Do half an exercise, borrow a suggestion, tweak an idea.
Write wherever and however you see fit.
Take what you want, when you want it...and leave the rest.

SIGNPOSTS

Tabs can be found along the outside edge of many pages. Brief phrases are written there.

These signposts do not tell you what the exercise is about.
They do not tell you everything you will learn.
They do not tell you all you need to know.

They can, however, help you to apply the techniques according to your needs. If you find yourself uncertain of where to turn when working on a scene or a moment, follow the signposts.

character creation:
This exercise focuses on discovering details about a figure(s) in our plays.

setting:
The where, when, maybe even a little of the how.

plot development:
Story, Story, Story. What happened?

power dynamics:
How do our characters get what they want and who do they bump up against during these efforts?

structure:
How is this different from plot development? Here, we are less concerned with what the story is than how it is told. What style can effectively tell this tale? What must happen midway through the play to insure that the ending is earned? Sometimes we explore the shape of an entire play. Sometimes, we focus in on a single scene.

making connections:
A little bit from over there, a dash from right here and a pinch from somewhere else. We pull from disparate areas and bring them together to create something new.

rewriting:
We tackle the play again.

THE BEGINNING

Begin: v.; To discover.

ON (NOT) FIGURING IT OUT

Before I even start on my path, I can weigh the value of taking this road or that.
I can calculate the trajectory.
I can estimate the velocity.
I can figure out the safest or fastest or most exciting route.

But I cannot plan what may happen along the journey.

The blacktop may turn bumpy.
The ground may break open and swallow me whole.
The sun may shine so bright that I have to stop and bask in it for an unexpected moment.

We don't have to know where we are headed.
We don't have to figure out how to get to that mysterious place.
We only have to begin.

LOOSEN UP

JOURNAL

I start my day with three or so pages of journaling.
I begin with a one page gratitude list.
What am I thankful for?
What is going right in my life?
What is difficult, from which I am learning much needed lessons?
Who am I thrilled to know?

I take two pages to work through my resentments and anything blocking the channel. I may even get out some of my rage. This is great training for the playwriting to come. Let it rip and let it go.

FEEL

Cry for ten minutes.
Scream for ten minutes.
Laugh for ten minutes.
I wish I could tell you how to make these things happen. I can't.
I can, however, guarantee that we all have something to grieve, we all have something to rail against, and we all have something that gives us joy.

MEDITATE

I sit quietly for at least ten minutes.
I watch my breathing, in and out.
My mind supposedly empties (not usually, but that's the spirit).
It gets quiet because it's about to get loud once again.

Some days, the playmaking starts from here.
Some days, I stop and eat breakfast.
Some days, I have business to attend to first.
Some days, no matter what I do, I can't get settled.

Everyday, however, no matter how rocky the transition into writing, I do begin.

THE CHARACTER CREATION VISUALIZATION
[do not skip—good stuff below!]

I know when I see the term "visualization" my first instinct is to skip ahead, searching for something with more tangible results.

The following exercises, however, are an integral part of the process and will come into play again and again.

This technique places us in a meditative, channel-worthy state while also teaching us a great deal about our characters in a concise way. You may find it helpful at any time, but especially when working with a new figure or scenario.

Close your eyes.
Imagine yourself in the body of your character.

Ask yourself (as the character) these questions:

1.)   How do I stand—tall and proud or slumped over and bent?
2.)   Is my skin taut and firm or is it sagging off the bones?
3.)   Am I bald or do I have luxurious hair?
4.)   Are my hands calloused or are they soft and well manicured?
5.)   My feet/shoes—soles worn out on one side or shined to a high finish?
6.)   What is the smell I most adore?
7.)   What is the sound I hate?
8.)   What makes me laugh?
9.)   Do I have children? If so, who's my favorite? If not, do I wish I did?
10.)   What is my most painful memory?
11.)   What has been my greatest loss?
12.)   Who do I love the most?
13.)   Who do I wish would leave me alone?
14.)   Who is the person closest to me in the world?
15.)   What is my biggest secret?
16.)   What is my biggest regret?
17.)   If I could achieve one unrealized dream, what would it be?
18.)   Where would I like to go that I have never been to?
19.)   If I could regain one moment, which would it be?
20.)   What have I forgotten?
21.)   What do I wish I'd forgotten?
22.)   What leaves me feeling bereft, with not a thing?
23.)   What fills me?
24.)   For what do I need to be forgiven?
25.)   What do I refuse to forgive?

26.)   Whom do I wish I could see one more time?
27.)   Do I like to dance?
28.)   Where in my body do I carry ache?
29.)   What is my greatest sin?
30.)   What am I an expert in?

Open your eyes.

You now know more about your character than most playwrights know after working for months. Feel free to make notes about some of the answers to these questions.

Mostly, though, trust that this information is in your bones...and get to writing.

GATES OF HEAVEN

On the first day of a playwriting seminar, I often follow the Character Creation Visualization with this simple but surprisingly profound exercise, inspired by an improvisational acting game.

Your character is at the Gates of Heaven. She has to convince St. Peter (or whatever figure is there according to your character's beliefs) to let her in.

The catch: she believes she has committed some great sin. A sin can be something as large as murder or as small as ignoring a friendly neighbor.

This is all about what your character BELIEVES to be unforgivable.

But, she also has an expertise. An expertise can be something as complicated as surgery or as common as denial. Take your pick.

In this MONOLOGUE, your character must use her expertise to overcome the weight of the sin:

> *You know, it's true, I slashed many tires in my day. Tried to prevent anyone from getting anywhere. Anywhere but here... with me. But, let me tell ya' fella, I can make a mean pie. And, if anyone had stuck around, the brown sugar on their tongue would have shown them greater love than they would have found anywhere else. And they would have been at peace. So, you see, let me in...*

Remember to use as many details as you can to make your case.

> *I used whole wheat flour on the pie's crusts, so that they would know I care—the filling was Granny Smith, not that pre-packaged, pre-canned shit—oh, excuse my language...*

15–20 minutes.

When you are done, read it over. You will have found out what makes this character tick and who she becomes in the face of great need.

You may have also discovered the seeds of her story, which will continue to reveal itself as the process continues.

THE SPACE VISUALIZATION

This can follow the Character Creation Visualization and/or can be used to help set any scene.

Close your eyes. Imagine yourself in the body of the character.

Ask:

1.)   Where am I?
2.)   Is it cold and damp or is it warm and dry?
3.)   Am I outside or in?
4.)   What is the quality of the light?
5.)   Does this place have a specific purpose?
6.)   Are the walls grimy or pristine?
7.)   What does the place smell like?
8.)   What are some objects in the space?
9.)   Can I touch them or are they just out of reach?
10.)   Which objects do I wish to avoid?
11.)   How do I feel about this place?
12.)   Is this place familiar or foreign?
13.)   What memories does this space contain?

PLACING ANOTHER CHARACTER IN THE SPACE

Stay in your meditative state and ask:

1.)   How close is the person physically to me?
2.)   How do I feel about his proximity?
3.)   Do I find this person attractive or repulsive?
4.)   Do I wish this person would go away or come nearer?
5.)   In what ways does this person scare me?
6.)   What do I wish to know about this person?
7.)   What do I wish to keep hidden from this person?
8.)   What is the one thing this person could give me that I do not have?
9.)   What is the one thing I refuse to give to this person?
10.)   What button do I know to push?
11.)   What button does this other person know to push?
12.)   What am I willing to give to this other?
13.)   What will I fight for with every ounce of my being?
14.)   Do I love this person or hate her?

You now know your character, the exact setting he is in and the most obvious teammate or antagonist he has in this moment. Start here.

THE FIRST SCENE

Let's not worry about getting folks talking to one another just yet.

We'll get them in the same space, interacting, staking their claims to power, showing who's boss and expressing needs in some form.

Because of the Space Visualization exercise, your two figures are already in a location. You also have a pretty clear picture of the nature of their relationship.

This will be a STAGE DIRECTIONS only scene.

1.)   Write down Character A's first stage direction.

         Alan reaches for the toothpaste tube.

2.)   Write down Character B's immediate action response.

         Ulysses twists the cap for Alan.

Now skip two pages.

4.)   Write down Character A's last stage direction.

         Alan punches the wall and exits.

5.)   Write down Character B's action response.

         Ulysses falls to the toilet and gags himself.

6.)   Fill the two pages in the middle with whatever directions you see fit.

> You can go very precise, outlining the tiny steps of each character's physical journey:
>
> *Alan lifts his arm an inch.*
> *Ulysses waves his pinky...*
>
> Or you can go wild:
> *Ulysses makes a rocket ship.*
> *They travel to the moon...*

Wherever you go, however, make sure you connect back to those final stage directions in some kind of organic way.

20 minutes.

setting

power dynamics

structure

character creation

THE FIRST DIALOGUE

I'm a writer.

I hate admitting the following:
I have trouble getting people to talk to each other on the page.
I'm afraid of making things too obvious.
Or too mysterious.
Or too unnatural.
Or too natural.
Or too...

This is how I get out of my own way.

MONOLOGUE 1

1.) Character A wants to kill Character B.
2.) He also wants Character B to empathize with his plight.
He will do and say whatever it takes to be understood.

> *Shirley, this Glock 9 mm pointed at your nose hurts me more than it hurts you. My hand is shaking, can't you see that? I would not do this unless I had no choice. Your life or mine. Do you forgive me?*

3.) By the end, the character either commits the act or gives up in exasperation and surrenders.

15 minutes.

MONOLOGUE 2

power dynamics

Forget the above scenario. This monologue should stand on its own.

1.) Character B wants Character A to leave her alone.
2.) She also wants Character A to empathize with her annoyance, her frustration with him. In other words, she wants to be understood.
3.) By the end, Character B has given up or keeps fighting.

15 minutes.

DIALOGUE

making connections

1.) Pull ten lines from monologue 1. Label them 1–10.
2.) Pull ten lines from monologue 2. Label them 1–10.

You may only use the twenty chosen lines.

> They should follow each other in sequence:
> *Character A says his line 1.*
> *Character B says her line 1.*
> *Character A says her line 2.*
> *Character B says her line 2.*

And so on.

10 minutes.

Read it.

Are your characters talking past one another?
Are they not listening?
Are they each only interested in their own needs?

Sounds a little like life.

character creation

power dynamics

making connections

character creation

NEWS OF THE DAY

We all have themes and stories that resonate with us at certain points in our lives. If you have any idea what your play "is" at this juncture, you may find this exercise helpful as a means of discovering a new way into your interests—a surprising line, a truthful monologue, an outrageous action. Save this scene and use its elements if and when needed.

Beg, borrow and steal. Even from ourselves.

If you do not yet know the nature of your piece, this may give you a new idea.

plot development

1.)   Choose five news stories that interest you. The more bizarre the better.
2.)   Choose one.
3.)   Choose who, from that story, your main character will be.
        Keep in mind that this figure might never appear in the actual news text, but plays a role nonetheless. For example, if the headline is *"Doctor finds new use for leeches,"* you may choose to have a *patient* receiving the leech treatment as your main figure.
4.)   Write a one to two page monologue where the protagonist is trying desperately to meet a need.

        Give me the big fat leech and take away my pain.

        Take 10 minutes to write this monologue.
5.)   Now, break down your character's story into five sentences.

> *A vampire bit Clara's neck.*
> *Clara tries to find a medicinal cure for the bite.*
> *She finally turns to leeches after nothing else works.*
> *She loses pints of blood and is declared legally dead.*
> *She is resurrected by the vampire...and they live happily ever after.*

7.)   Look at the last sentence. Write a scene based on it.
8.)   Do the same with the first sentence.
9.)   You now have a first scene and a last. In the middle you will put the monologue.
10.)   Go back and add any stage directions you see fit.

                                                                        60 minutes

You will probably have in front of you a great model for theatrical storytelling:

Step 1: We meet the character and find out pertinent info quickly.

Step 2: Blatant need expressed and an action-oriented attempt to get that need met. Desperation at a non-achievement of the goal set up in step one.

making connections

Step 3: Resolution. The character has come to some new place. The need has
been met or its lack of fulfillment forgiven.

As always, you may now tweak and turn and twist to help the story make more sense.
Or you may find that the second act, the monologue, is a small example of the kind of
struggle your character must go through over and over again throughout the course of
the piece. You can start here with your play.

character creation

plot development

making connections

ESSENCES

My own monologues often take their whole length to find what their characters are really trying to express. How can I then, after getting through one, go back and find the truth?

Look over any monologue you have written.
Choose twenty words. Some may carry great weight (names, places, emotional states). Others may not. Lean more on the heavy words.

Write the monologue once more.
This time, you may only use the twenty selected words to tell the same story. Do not worry if details are missed. The emotional journey will be clear.

> A brief example:
> *I was born in Mississippi and I never cried, not until the air hit my teeth. Three years later.*
>
> Chosen Words: born, Mississippi, never, cried, hit, later
> *Born Boooooooorrrrrrnnnnn. Mississippi. Miss–iss–ippi. Cried. Never. Cried. Never. Never Cried. Never never nev-*
> *er.*
> *Later.*
> *Later.*
> *Later.*
> *HIT.*
> *CRIIIIIEEEEEDDD!*

10 minutes.

20.

SCENE COMPOSITION

This exercise was inspired by a staging technique called composition in which all participants are encouraged to serve as director/author/creators. Use of this tool in varying degrees can be found in the ensemble-created work of such companies as *Tectonic Theatre Project*, *Complicite*, and *Siti*. If any of these folks come to town, check 'em out.

1.)   Choose a few favorite quotes that seem to reflect your developing play's themes or general struggles and questions. These can be famous quotes, citations from Shakespeare, bits of well-known speeches, etc.

2.)   Choose three or four objects that appear in the setting of your play or that a character might have used at some point in his/her life.

3.)   Make a list of themes.

> Below are some I have used in the past:
> *How do we try to escape?*
> *How do we celebrate?*
> *How do we mourn?*
> *How long can I hold on?*
> *What will it take to let go?*
> *At some point, we have all wanted to die.*
> *I wish I was somebody else.*
> *I wish I had the answers.*
> *Come here...Go away.*
> *I will never give in.*

Feel free to add your own.

4.)   Make a list of contrasting elements.

> *High and low.*
> *Slow and fast.*
> *Deep and shallow.*
> *Rough and smooth.*
> *Chaos and order.*
> *Joy and despair.*
> *Silence and noise.*

Once again, add your own.

5.)   Choose one of the listed themes.

> A good one to start with:
> *How do we try to escape?*

setting

making connections

6.)   The First Composition scene must reverberate on that theme and include:
        At least two characters.
        At least three of the contrasting elements from your list.
        A moment of violence.
        A moment of song.
        An object you have chosen.
        One of the quotes.

Other than making sure those elements are incorporated, this is an open space for you to find out about your characters and their stories.

                                                                    20 minutes.

THE SECOND SCENE COMPOSITION

The first time I rode a bike it was awkward. My feet sometimes fell behind the tire's increasing speed. The next time, I was more successful, able to keep a steady pace.

Let's try again.

1.)   Choose one theme:
                I wish I had the answers.

2.)   Choose a new quote.
        Choose a new object.
        At least three of the contrasting elements.
        A moment of dance.
        A frozen moment.
        Laughter.

                                                                    20 minutes.

Continue to add to your contrast and theme lists.

Do this exercise whenever the ideas are coming, but you don't know what shape they wish to take. You will probably find that you can create a number of the scenes in your play with this easy and fun method.

setting

making connections

DREAM A LITTLE DREAM

Our dream lives reveal a great deal about our passions, our fantasies and, perhaps most of all, our fears.

This variation on the composition scene will reveal that which is inherently theatrical.

The visualizations from earlier in the chapter may help you to get into the necessary creative space.

1.)   Make a list of five places your character has been. These can be as exotic as Barbados or as simple as the grocery store down the street.
2.)   Make a list of five people your character has met or knows well. These can be as filled with history as parents or as inconsequential as the newspaper boy who delivers the morning paper.
3.)   And lastly, make a list of five fears your character has. These can be as tangible as a monster under the bed or as intangible as a fear of abandonment.
4.)   You will write a dream sequence for your character:
All five figures must appear, even if only for a moment.
One character must suddenly transform into a different chararcter.
All five locations must appear, even if only for a moment.
One location must suddenly transform into a different location.
All five fears must occur. (*Now, this is open to interpretation, especially for the intangible ones. They can all happen at the same time—the monster appears while a parent is abandoning—or be separated by pages of action.*)

If in doubt about how to begin, start with this stage direction:

> *Character A opens his eyes.*
> *He is sitting in...*

30 minutes.

ON STRUCTURE

Every life is unique.
Each human lives her own story in her own way.
But, every person is born.
Every person has experiences that happen after birth.
And every person dies.
Such is the structure of life.

Every play has its own structure.
The details and how they unfold are unique to our pieces, to our characters' journeys.
We can, however, trust that there are modes of storytelling which carry truths.
We can learn from these structures and allow them to teach us about our plays.

MYTH MAKING

Myths carry structures that move and inspire us. By looking at how they work, we may learn something about storytelling.

Choose a myth (or a famous work that has reached mythic status, *Macbeth*, for example) that resonates on themes meaningful to you.

1.)   Once you have chosen a myth you know well, write down the story as simply as you can in three paragraphs.

2.)   Look at that first paragraph.

> Orpheus, the music maker, marries his love Eurydice. She dies soon after, descending to Hades. In his grief, Orpheus vows to retrieve her from the underworld and sets off on his journey.

3.)   Write this paragraph as a scene. If you find that it covers too much ground, feel free to use just the first sentence or two as your jumping off point.

                                                                    15 minutes.

4.)   Look at that last paragraph.

> Orpheus sings a lament over his lost love, Eurydice. The Bacchae appear and chop off his head. The head continues wailing as it sails down the river.

5.)   Write this paragraph as a scene. The same guidelines apply, only this time, feel free to use just the LAST sentence or two as your starting place.

                                                                    15 minutes.

Read it over.

Is the contrast between the beginning and ending apparent or does it feel strangely circular?

Does the ending, in relation to the beginning, carry a wallop of surprise or a sadness of inevitability?

And, most importantly, what about this basic structure moves you?

structure

25.

REWRITING THE MYTH

Utilizing the Myth Making work you have already accomplished, refer to the last paragraph in your three-paragraph structure.

1.)   Rewrite it so that the myth ends in a way that feels opposite to the original.

> *Orpheus cries his lamentation to the Gods. Eurydice returns to life and beckons to her love. They move to a cabin in the woods. They sing to one another for eternity.*

2.)   Once you have completed that task, write this paragraph as a scene.

30 minutes

Read that new ending scene.

Does it feel false? Probably. But does it also feel possible? Probably.

As writers, we are presented with choices, big ones, little ones, but some carry resonance and others are just "figuring it out."

structure

BORROWING FROM THE MASTERS

We turn once again to those who came before us.

1.) Choose a play you know, preferably a classic—think *Hamlet, Miss Julie, Hedda Gabler.*
2.) Write down the story of the play in essay form. This may take a few pages.
3.) Break down that essay into only ten sentences which tell the most important elements of the story in chronological order.
4.) Write down the story of *your* play. You don't have to know what the story is yet. Make it up and you may discover it along the way!
5.) Break it down into ten sentences.
6.) Now find a way to place the elements from sentence one of your play and place them in the context of sentence one of the classic—in other words, use the classic structure to tell your story.

> Sentence one of my play:
>
> *Theresa consumes her body and throws up her heart.*
>
> Sentence one of the classic:
>
> *Hamlet returns home only to discover that his father has died and so, he mourns.*
>
> The combined sentence:
>
> *Theresa returns home to discover that her body has died and she, in her own way, mourns.*

7.) Read the combined sentence and WRITE THAT SCENE.

15 minutes

You may do this for EVERY SENTENCE along the way.

> Sentence five of my play:
>
> *Theresa's husband Sam returns to the hospital, fearing it is time to remove Theresa's feeding tube.*
>
> Sentence five of the classic:
>
> *Hamlet contemplates killing Claudius, but decides against it, afraid his stepfather will go to heaven, absolved.*
>
> The combined sentence:
>
> *Sam returns to the hospital to kill Theresa, but decides against it, afraid that she will leave him alone, her soul absolved.*

plot development

structure

making connections

Spend no more than 15 minutes on each scene. This does not have to be done in a single session; you may return to this exercise over a period of days, allowing yourself quick and intense bursts of discovery.

Once you have completed the process, you will find that you have a quick sketch of an entire piece that hews to a classic structure and gives you a great jumping off point for writing your play.

If you find you are having difficulty with the above assignment, here are some practical tips:

1.) Make a list of characters for "your play" and for the "classic." See if you can find equivalent figures. For example:

	My play	Classic
Best Friend	Arnie	Horatio
Nemesis	Alfie	Claudius

2.) Get out of your own way. Trust that your mind and heart will stretch to put order on the chaos and if nothing else, you will wind up with a creative muscle strengthening exercise.

plot development

structure

making connections

LOST OBJECTS

This is a variation on the structure of a classic hero's journey. Think *Peer Gynt* or Homer's *Odyssey*.

This exercise will help you construct an entire play, in miniature, which may serve as a rough outline for the piece you are discovering.

By focusing on the quest for an object, your characters will be motivated with concrete needs.

1.)   Begin with your Character Creation Visualization.
2.)   Then go through the Space Visualization.
3.)   Place your character in the space, and begin the journey.

ACT ONE

1.)   Your main character has possession of some object. In no more than one page, Character A speaks of the object's beauty and its meaning.
2.)   The object is then in some way lost.

> Think theatrically.
> *A wire drops from above and plucks the object away.*
>
> Or think commonplace.
> *Another character snatches it from him and exits abruptly.*

ACT TWO

1.)   Character A begins the search. The first part of this act includes an attempt to retrieve the object while not leaving the space. Your character searches every-where. Perhaps he yells and screams, throws a tantrum or jumps high into the sky trying to get it back. Nothing works.
2.)   He leaves the space and automatically finds himself in a brand new location. This can be a huge change:

> *from classroom to outer space.*

3.)   Another figure (Character B) appears. She has a new object she wants A to take. She will do whatever it takes:

> *seduction, cajoling, begging.*

4.)   Character A refuses and exits with Character B hot on his heels.
5.)   A new location:

> *from outer space to a jungle.*

29.

plot development

power dynamics

structure

Character A continues his search while encountering new barriers:

leaves, rain, darkness.

6.)   Character B has caught up and tries to force, through violence, her object
onto our protagonist, who struggles to escape her clutches and continue forward
in his search.

ACT TWO EXTENDED

7.)   One more location. New characters appear. In this setting, however, no one can
hear anyone else. A asks for help in finding his object. The others ask for help in
finding things they have lost. Everyone speaks; no one listens.

8.)   Character B, ever persistent, still tries to get A to take the damn object.
B might try loud pleading, like so many of the other characters. She could also
get clever and try mime.

9.)   The scene concludes in one of the following ways:
In frustration, A kills B and leaves the object.
A surrenders and accepts B's replacement object.
A escapes B and the new object is forgotten.
A escapes B and comes across his old object in a simple way. For example:

It's waiting for him on the ground.

ACT THREE

1.)   A returns to his original location.
Everything remains the same. The only change is that he now has the object in
hand.

OR everything is different, Character B's object now in his possession, and he is
unsure of what to do.

OR he is without any object and feeling utterly dejected.

OR he is without any object and full of hope.

End of Play.

60 minutes.

plot development

power dynamics

structure

30.

ON STAMINA

Stamina: (n.) Strength of physical constitution; power to endure disease and fatigue.

Writing a play demands stamina.
It beckons.
It calls.
It begs.
It pleads.
For you to keep going, no matter what.

On average, I write roughly one play per year. That doesn't mean I don't start five. (I do and soon discover that one of them is the piece that I work through and it rewards by working me in return.) It doesn't mean I love every page. It doesn't mean my first draft is also my last.

It means that I don't stop, even when nothing is coming.
I listen.
I observe.
I write through the pain, the doubt, the anger, the fear, the resentment, the boredom.

We have, up to this point, performed many tasks of written discovery.
Some have been complex in their psychological and structural challenges.
Some have been quick.
Others have taken up more time.
These tasks must continue.
Some, such as the next, will go longer and deeper.
Some will touch lightly.
All will depend on you.

Stamina: (n.) Derived from Stamen, the life threads of the Fates.

THE SEVEN MERITORIOUS PRACTICES PLAY

I take it on faith that a writer's job is merely to channel his characters' experiences and conflicts, and thus, drama will automatically rise. Our only responsibility is to know our characters' darkest corners intimately, exploring and exploding these hidden places.

The following is based on a Buddhist prayer meditation known as "The Seven Meritorious Practices." For more information on the details of this daily experience, I recommend The Dalai Lama's *How to Practice*.

HOMAGE: (n.) RESPECT OR REVERENCE

1.) Do the Character Creation Visualization.
2.) In monologue form, Character A will thank someone for some positive action she has taken. The unseen Character B will continually refuse to accept this gratitude. Character A, however, needs her gratitude to be heard and acknowledged.
The monologue must include:
One moment of laughter.
A Dance.
A Scream.

15 minutes.

RITUAL: (n) A SYSTEM OF RITES

This is a stage directions only sequence, similar to **THE FIRST SCENE** on page 14, but with a greater focus on the power dynamics at play between your two characters.

1.) Do the Space Visualization.
2.) Characters A and B are in a familiar space performing some fairly mundane ritual.

> *In the bathroom, brushing teeth. In the kitchen, preparing dinner...*

3.) Write Character A's first action.
4.) Write Character B's immediate action response.
5.) Skip two pages.
6.) Write Character A's last action.
7.) Write Character B's immediate action response.
8.) Fill in the middle with directions that are minute and precise:

> *A squeezes the tail end of the tube.*

or wild and big:

> *B travels to the moon, fire trailing behind him.*

32.

This ritual should reveal something about your characters' relationship.

> Who has higher status and when does he use it?
> *A moves toward the door.*
> *B gets on his knees and pulls at A's apron.*
> *A kicks her heel into B's face.*

20 minutes.

ILL DEEDS — ILL: (adj.) OF UNSOUND PHYSICAL OR MENTAL HEALTH

All too often, we view our protagonists as flawless folks with a penchant for heroic deeds. They are human beings, with quirks and foibles—and that is what makes them beautiful.

1.) We see Character A engage in performing an ill deed.

   a lie, a murder, an unkind action

2.) There should be at least one other character in the space whom this is impacting, Character C.

3.) Be aware that Character A wishes to be understood. In other words, she desires that Character C forgives and/or agrees with her deed and A will do what she needs to to make this happen.

If you are struggling with the open structure of this step, here's a helpful tip:

1.) Write the first line of dialogue for this scene.

> For example, you might start with the line:
> *I don't mean to hurt you, but...*

2.) Skip one page. Write a stage direction.
3.) Skip one page. Write the last line of dialogue.
4.) Fill in the middle.

15 minutes

ADMIRATION: (n.) AN OBJECT OF WONDER

Same as above, except this time we see our protagonist performing a positive action.

   giving to charity, comforting someone, forgiving

A new character (D), who this is affecting, might be introduced.

If you want to complicate the motivations a bit, be aware of your character's desire to see her positive action recognized. What steps might your protagonist take in an effort

character creation

structure

making connections

to insure that this moment is seen and appreciated?

15 minutes.

ENTREATY: (n.) AN EARNEST REQUEST OR PLEADING

1.) Character A must convince one of the characters to give him something.

> This could be something tangible:
>
> *a car, money...*
>
> or something more abstract:
>
> *absolution, love...*

The other character continually denies the request.
This should be a dialogue/stage direction scene and should include:
A Moment of Crying
A Tantrum
Begging
One moment of profanity

2.) The scene should reach a crescendo where the character attempts to perform all actions at once.

> *Character A cries and pounds her fists while screaming, 'You asshole, I beg you...'*

3.) When that fails:
One simple statement of what the need is. No more than one sentence.
The other character either accepts or denies the request.
End Scene

20 minutes.

SUPPLICATION: (n.) AN ACT OF HUMILITY

1.) Character A is alone.
Character A causes him/herself harm.
2.) Write down one simple action of self-harm (could also be a harming piece of dialogue).
3.) What came right before that simple action?
Write that in no more than five sentences, dialogue and/or stage direction.
4.) What comes after the action?
How does your character recover/clean up/fix the proceeding action?
Write that in no more than five sentences, dialogue and/or stage direction.

10 minutes.

DEDICATION: (n.) A WHOLE AND EARNEST DEVOTION

A monologue.
No one else is on stage.

Character A dedicates her life, everything we have seen come before in the play, to those who she has met along the way.
This should include a moment of thanks.
At least one object from a previous scene.
At least one moment of the ritual.
End with a prayer.

20 minutes.

Your character began from a place of need and ended in a place of acceptance, however grudgingly, a very full arc.

You can now use this as the basic structure for a larger piece, exploding some of the scenes into larger formats. If nothing else, you have learned a great deal about your character.

ON TACTICS

When in doubt about what your character may choose to do next, turn to any of these actions. They can take away your blocks and get the characters moving in unexpected ways.

If you're lucky, the actions below will reveal your story and its dynamics:

Sing	Cite statistics	
Dance	Pull hair	Masturbate
Scream	Punch	Blow something up
Cry	Kick	Have sex
Lie	Shoot himself	Seduce
Tell the truth	Stab herself	Brush teeth
Beg	Deny	Run away
Bark	Juggle	Lean close
Meow	Laugh	Ask a question
Hiss	Tell a joke	Propose marriage
Curse	Cite a memory	Smash something
Apologize	Stroke someone's arm	Rip it to shreds
Make up a word	Pat an ass	Threaten with death

Add your own as well...

TACTICAL USES

As you do any of the exercises in this book you may use the tactics to make the crafted scenes even more action oriented.

1.)   Choose three tactics.
2.)   Choose a writing exercise from anywhere in the book.
3.)   The resulting scene must include your choices, even if they are thrown in randomly.

You may not wind up keeping the selections in the final draft, but your characters will have to deal with a large action taken swiftly and unexpectedly.

We will find out who your folks become in the face of need and desire that are expressed blatantly.

character creation

power dynamics

MUSICAL...THE MUSICAL!

In musicals, words are often sung when the characters have reached an emotional peak, where mere prose will no longer suffice.

1.)   Choose two styles of music.
        One that perfectly fits the mood you are in.
        The other should be the exact opposite in tone and content.

          Heavy Metal vs. Easy Listening

2.)   Set the scene:

          A bedroom.
          Character A wishes to have sex.
          Character B wishes to fall asleep.

3.)   Character A must use at least five tactics to get the wish.
        Character B must use at least three tactics to resist.

4.)   They will reach a stalemate.

SING OUT LOUISE!

5.)   Character A will break into song in the style of your mood.
        This song will express everything that Character A has left unsaid.

6.)   Character B will give in.

          They begin to have sex.

7.)   Character B will stop for some reason (loss of interest, fear...).

8.)   Character A will attempt to continue.

CRESCENDO!

9.)   This struggle will reach a stalemate and Character B will break into song in an attempt to get Character A to stop.
        This song will be in the style that is the opposite in tone and content.
        Character B will express everything that has been left unsaid.

10.)   Character A will respond in his style.

11.)   Character B then in her style.
        And on and on.

By the end, the song will either have become chaos and the characters are driven apart.
OR
They are singing a duet in perfect harmony—a coming together.

                                                            60 minutes

power dynamics

structure

VERSE AND PROSE

The same kind of thing can be done with verse and prose.

Instead of music, use iambic pentameter *(10 syllables of alternating unstressed and stressed sounds: "But soft! What light through yonder window breaks?")* and slang.

1.)   Put any two characters in a high stakes situation.
2.)   Have one character reach a crescendo and then speak in pentameter.
3.)   The other character will speak in high-impact slang.
       The use of profanity in its many permutations is encouraged.
4.)   They will either find a way to work together or burst apart.

30 minutes.

Either of these exercises can also be used late in the play development process. When you have created a scene where everyone sounds alike or where a peak is not reached effectively, try these out.

Then, use the created scene as an outline for the emotional shape of your play's missing moment.

structure

making connections

THE CHILD INSIDE

WARNING!
This exercise has been deemed "touchy-feely" by some!
I encourage you to use it in whatever way you see fit. I have seen some highly comic scenes emerge from this, and some gentle, touching ones.

You can do this with any character of your choosing. As always, if you do not yet have a consistent character you are working with, feel free to use the Character Creation Visualization.

1.)   Your character finds himself in a familiar place.
2.)   In stage direction, take at least half a page to explore what is going on here. Where is he? What is he trying to get?
   What is in his way?

> *Character A is in a bedroom. There is a twin bed and a boy band poster, circa 1982. A rips the poster off the wall. He looks at the wall closely, searching.*
> *A then moves to the bed.*
> *Turns over the mattress. Looks at the box spring, searching.*

3.)   He comes across some object.

> *Eureka! A picture falls out from behind the headboard. He places it gingerly in his hands.*

4.)   In some magical way that object calls forth a child.

> *As he does so, a child appears in spotlight, identical to the image in the picture.*

The child is the young version of the character you are working with.
5.)   The child wants to play a game. The child will do whatever it takes to get what he wants. This may include insulting the older version of himself,

> *"What happened to you? You got fat!"*

6.)   The adult character just wants the kid to shut the heck up and leave him alone. He will do whatever he has to in order for this to happen.
7.)   By the end of the scene, the child has gotten his wishes, has been abandoned or has been killed.

30 minutes.

This scene has helped you find who your character is on the inside—what has been lost and what could still be regained.

15 MINUTES TO LIVE

Any character you may imagine.
Do this here.
Do this later.
Do it when you are stuck.
Do it when you've lost your way.
Do it when you're bored.
Do it.

1.) Your character is about to die.
  Perhaps he is about to lose his grip from a collapsing bridge.
  Or, he is about to stick a knife in his own heart.
  Whatever the case, he has only 15 minutes to live.
2.) Another person appears.
3.) He must tell this person his life's story with the remaining time.
  He will tell the parts that are important.
  He will leave off the parts that aren't.
  He will share that which must not be forgotten.
  He will forget that which can be.
  His story may span twenty years.
  Or it may encompass only the last twenty seconds.
  What is his life and how does he tell it?

15 minutes.

When you are done, you will know what must, for this person's tale to be told, be put on the stage.

You will know what should be left out.

structure

character creation

plot development

making connections

FORGET THE PAST

A lot of plays have that monologue where someone tells an important story from their past. He remembers a particular moment in his childhood. She recalls when a gun was held against her head.

Your characters have these important moments. You may want to share them.

Don't share them in the past. Share them here. Share them now.

1.)   Place your character in a life threatening situation.

> *He is being robbed at knife-point.*
> *She is sitting in an airplane about to crash.*

2.)   Instead of telling his life story, as in the earlier exercise, he will tell the story of what is happening right now. Moment by moment. Beat by beat.

> Physical sensations:
> *My side aches as the sharp point pierces my flesh.*

> Emotional states:
> *I am scared. So scared that I can't see anything.*
> *Just white light.*

> Desires:
> *I just want it to end. When will it end?*

> Things others say:
> *"Are you okay?"*

> Fleeting thoughts:
> *"What a question."*

3.)   Start in one state:

> *detachment, surprise, fear*

4.)   End in the opposite place:

> *alertness, acceptance, love*

5.)   Fill in the middle with every step of the emotional journey. Let your character surprise you. She may cross through despair which paralyzes, followed by joyful celebration.

The human heart can beat erratically, but it still keeps us breathing.

15 minutes

FACING FEARS

What is the character you are working with afraid of?
It could be as tangible as snakes.
It could be as intangible as dishonesty. *(If you go this route, make it specific:* "My char-
acter must lie to save a life.")

Your figure will be faced with this fear and will have no choice but to deal with it.

> Character A's wife holds a gun to her head.
> Wife: Did you cheat on me?

At first your figure will resist in every way.
He will say nothing.
He will say too much.
He will hit.
He will shut his eyes and close his ears.
He will run.

Somehow, by the end of the scene, he will come to embrace this fear, to love it, to be
grateful for what it has given him.
OR
He will crumple.
He will die.
The fear will overwhelm him and the worst possible outcome will take place.

25 minutes

character creation

plot development

power dynamics

character creation

plot development

structure

THE STAGES OF GRIEF

One day, a student *(thanks Kellie)* talked to me about a character who was struggling with letting go of her dying mother. She spoke about the character going through the Kubler–Ross stages of grief, but wasn't sure how to proceed. This is the resulting exercise.

This technique is not exclusive to death and grief scenes. It can be used for any situation where a character is trying desperately to hold on or is refusing to accept any kind of loss.

MONOLOGUE

Character A is in the process of experiencing a loss.
Perhaps, a father is dying, a lover is leaving or a favorite pint of ice cream is almost empty.

1.)   Set the stage. Two lines of stage direction.

> *Character A stands at the open freezer.*
> *A pint of ice cream in his hands.*

Before you begin the monologue, always remember that a character is in NEED. So, in this case, you character's need is to hold on, to not let anything go.

2.)   The first 3–7 lines should be a DENIAL of the situation.

> The denial should show up in the form of questions:
> *Where is the rest of the ice cream? Is it hiding?*

3.)   The next 5–10 lines will express ANGER in the form of blame:

> *You bastard pint, you always tease me. You're a liar.*
> *You're not rich and creamy enough anyway.*

4.)   The next 7–12 lines consists of BARGAINING:

> *If I put you back into the cold, you will give me sugary*
> *goodness.*

Let these bargaining points grow larger and more desperate as the sequence goes along. Character A may be willing to do some pretty outrageous things to get needs met.

44.

5.)   The next 10–20 lines will express DEPRESSION. Now, remember, depression
        is not sadness, it is numbness, a disconnection, a lack of feeling. In the section,
        CHARACTER A cannot feel and will try to convince the other figure to help him
        regain sensation.

> *Pour yourself on my tongue, every last bit, so I know you*
> *ain't goin' nowhere.*

This too should grow ever more desperate.

6.)   The final sequence is ACCEPTANCE. Character A clearly expresses the
        finality of the given loss.

> *I know you are almost gone. I will miss your refreshing*
> *flavor. Goodbye.*

45 minutes.

GRIEF IN ACTION

Stage direction only!

1.)   DENIAL — In action, this would best be expressed by an active pushing away of
        the undesirable information:

> *CHARACTER A turns the pint of ice cream upside down.*
> *Empty. She places it in the freezer. Shuts the door. Opens*
> *the door. Slams the door. Again and again and again.*

2.)   ANGER — Hurling accusation with objects:

> *Character A takes the ice cream bowl and throws it to the*
> *floor. It shatters!*

3.)   BARGAINING — Make offerings:

> *Character A grabs a container of cream. She kneels at the*
> *pint. Pours the contents of container into pint. Waits.*

4.)   DEPRESSION — Efforts to feel something:

> *A licks the inside of the pint. Taps on her tongue. Nothing.*
> *Licks again. Nothing. Bites a chunk of the pint container.*
> *Chews. Nothing.*

character creation

5.)   ACCEPTANCE — An action that clearly demonstrates an understanding of
       reality:

> *A places the pint in the garbage can. Closes the lid.*
> *Waves goodbye.*

30 minutes.

GIVING GRIEF

Combine the two grief exercises above.

Find where the action and words combined would have the greatest impact. Find where
the actions express more clearly than the language ever does. Find the truth and let it
rip.

plot development

structure

INANIMATE RELATIONS

Pick an inanimate item which has an intimate relationship with a person.
This item sees and hears the darkest moments and the most joyful private celebrations. Example: *This laptop computer.*

APPRECIATE ME!

Monologue
The object feels used.
It wants appreciation for the services it has provided.
It will do or say whatever it takes to get this acknowledgment.
This will probably include an airing of dirty laundry.
Remember, this object has witnessed some very sordid, vulnerable, secret acts.

10 minutes.

APPRECIATE ME TOO!

Monologue.
A supporting figure.
If you already know your play's characters, this might be the figure who is closest to your protagonist.
Or you can just pick from the usual litter: The Best Friend, The Lover, The Mother...
This character feels jealous of the object.
He/She wants to be appreciated as well.
Will do or say whatever it takes.
Also has lots of intimate knowledge. Uses it.
This figure may also destroy the object if the heat gets too high.

10 minutes.

I DON'T NEED NO THANKS

Monologue.
The character who is receiving all of this pleading finally has his say.
He defends himself. This defense is most effective when addressed to the fellow living person. Mainly, he wants to keep his power.

10 minutes.

INANIMATE INTIMACY

Sometimes I need to trick myself, finding ways into character conflict, which surprises me, the know–it–all creator.

A scene.
Use only the lines you have already written in the three preceding monologues.
Break them up as you see fit. You may choose a specific location where the characters are. Using only lines from the monologues, your human figures state their cases. The object may, at times, speak up, unheard by the humans.

OR

Again, a specific location.
All three figures, object included, interact, addressing one another directly.

OR

Set the scene in a consciously theatrical way.

> *An empty stage. Three spotlights. Our characters speak directly to the audience.*

Break up the monologues in such a way that the figures seem to reflect and comment on each other's words. They, however, never engage directly.

30 minutes.

If you do this again late in the process, you may find bits and pieces of your story (and also your characters' weak spots) you did not know you knew.

character creation

making connections

PEDESTRIAN/ABSTRACT

Often, good theatre consists of small moments blown up to epic proportions.

The theatre-maker Robert Wilson is especially good at this—someone's reaction to an event can take five minutes even if in "real life" 'twas just a one second eyebrow raise.

1.)   Take two characters and put them in a fairly usual everyday situation—in the kitchen preparing dinner or in the bathroom washing their faces before bed (see "Ritual" in the Seven Step Play). If these are characters you are already working with, make it as specific as you can to their lives as you know it.

2.)   Write ten lines that deal with these mundane details.
        This can be a combination of stage direction and dialogue.

3.)   At line eleven, something changes.

> This change may be small:
> *A's hand curls into a ball.*
>
> or something big:
> *All of Character A's teeth fall out.*
> or
> *Character B's stomach explodes.*

4.)   For the next twenty lines the characters spin further and further into abstraction. These abstractions may also be dialogic in nature.

> Maybe words are repeated, then drawn out until they are unrecognizable:
> *"Mellow*
> *Mellow*
> *Mellllloooowww*
> *Meeeeellllloooowwww*
> *Meeeellllooooooooooooooooooooooooooooooooooooooooooooooooooo*
> *ooooooooooooooooooooooooooooooooooooooooooooooooooooooooooooo*
> *owwwwwwwwwwwwwwwwwwwwwwwwwwwwww!"*

5.)   Then at line 31, your characters abruptly return to the pedestrian action and dialogue we started with. This continues for three to five lines.
        End scene.

                                                                        25 minutes.

I often find that this experiment mimics the experience of an inner journey. We see the turmoil, pain and comedy inside the small moments—also, talk about theatrical! Have fun!

49.

SAY IT, DO IT, LIVE IT

First rule about this exercise: Be obvious!

Second rule: Have fun!

You can do this with anywhere from 1 to 15 characters.
My suggestion—start out with two.

1.)   Characters A and B (and C and D and...) are each desperately trying to get
        something from one another.
        This scenario is almost always true.

        In this scene, every time a character does something, he/she says what is being
        done and why he/she is doing it:

> *Character A: I am moving this couch while straining mightily
>   so you will feel guilty about not helping.*
>
> *Character B: I am smoking this cigarette and blowing the
>   smoke in your eyes, so you will cry and I
>   will know that you can feel something.*

        And on and on.

2.)   This scene should reach a crescendo where each character is continually topping
        the other.
3.)   By the end, the characters have both collapsed in exhaustion.
        Or both have gone their separate ways.
        Or they come to some sort of agreement, by which I mean that one figure has
        probably gotten his/her way.

                                                                        25 minutes.

plot development

power dynamics

structure

50.

SAY IT AIN'T SO

Same premise as Say It, Do It, Live It.

This time you may have one character saying what the other character is doing and why she is doing it.

> Character A: *You are laughing because you want me to get upset.*
> Character B: *You are crying because you wish I was someone else and are trying to get me to change.*

And on and on.

At the end of either of these exercises, you will find that you have successfully laid out all the beats of a scene with clarity and purpose.

You can now go back and write a more "conventional" scene, using this as a kind of emotional outline for that which remains between the lines and is left unspoken.

If you're daring, leave this scene as is and stick it in a play. It will be a fun departure from the world of realism and into a heightened state, where the internal lives are revealed completely.

25 minutes.

plot development

power dynamics

structure

ON RESEARCH

We have poured a lot out.
Hopes, dreams, needs for forgiveness, pleas for yesterday and desires for tomorrow.
The well might be empty and it is time to fill it.

I know a lot about human struggles, joys, questions, needs, blocks, wounds...I'm not special.
We all do.
After all, we're human.

But there are also things I don't know. I don't know the exact temperature at which ethyl alcohol boils. I don't know how you insert a shunt into someone's brain. I don't know what it's like to study for the bar or to modify my body until it's unrecognizable. I don't know the experience of having my fingers freeze off or my heart stop. I don't know the feeling of having someone die in my arms and I don't know what it's like in Kenya in December. I don't know what Vine Street in Hollywood looked like in 1922 and I don't know what it's like to climb to the top of a tree in the middle of a thunder storm. I don't know how long a person can last without human contact. I don't know what it's like to perform in the Catskills and I don't know how my skin feels when I am trapped in an electrified box.

I don't know much of anything.

Here, in this process, is my opportunity to learn.
I look at all I have written.
I make lists of my characters' situations that I can't write effectively because my experience is lacking.
I make lists of questions.
I challenge myself to get curious about the answers.
I get humble and embrace this opportunity to become someone else, to walk in others' shoes, to travel far and feel unpleasant, frightened, beautiful, hellish, wonderful things.

THE INTERNET

What a great tool for gathering information!
I just type in a word and see what comes up.
What's cool about this method of research is the surprising places I may be led.

I can type in a term and wind up knee deep in a tangentially related topic. When I was writing my play, *McGoogle*, I was greatly interested in Timothy McVeigh. All I can tell you is that by researching on the internet, the play now includes whole passages about the Pope, stem cell research, the Miracle at Fatima and Muhammed Ali. The connections in this world are amazing and the internet can help you to see those ties.

BOOKS

If the internet is great for finding connections and quick bits of info, books are your greatest source for in-depth research. Dig deep. Read the relevant books and you will be surprised by how much depth enters the world of your play.

TALKING TO FOLKS

Talk to friends, talk to enemies, talk to lovers, talk to those who were there and those who heard about it.

Talk, but more importantly, listen! People will share interesting details, yes...but, and here's where you get lucky, they will share their opinions, fears and questions.

BEING THERE

If you can, physically go to the places that may appear in your piece or that, in some way, exist in the world of your play. When I was working on *Record Storm Spreads Ruin!*, a play about the Los Angeles Flood of 1938 and its political ramifications, I visited Clifton's Cafeteria in Los Angeles. This place, a fake redwood forest still serving 1950's style cuisine (think chipped beef) in the middle of Los Angeles, is amazing. What a setting! It now appears in the play as a representation of idealism in the corrupt noir world of 1930's Southern California.

Go out there and learn!

THE POWER OF THE GROUP

We have spent a lot of time. Alone.
We have written and we have written and we have written.
We have read and watched and visited. Alone.

Now I know writers often celebrate the power of isolation and romanticize the challenges of working alone in their little cocoons. I believe in this too and often practice the kind of solitude which can be helpful and necessary.

But it is time to fill the well with companionship, learning and sharing with fellow creators. After all, a group has power. It has energy and life and excitement and, above all, focus.

Every week, I teach numerous classes. In these classes, at least half of each three hour session is spent WRITING. Not talking, not analyzing, not criticizing—WRITING!

I encourage you to gather together with others who are working on a project or who just want to be engaged in the act of writing.
Once a week.
In your home.
Or a coffee shop.
Or, hell, in the garage.
For two or three hours.
Choose an exercise.
Give yourself a time constraint.
Work on it.
Read them to each other.
Write some more.
Read it.
Go home.
Next week—rinse and repeat.

If you do this on an ongoing basis, you will create a body of work. You will feel the pressure and joy of the group and get some words on the page. I don't usually make guarantees. But this time I will.

GROUP EXERCISES

To get started, I recommend doing something fun that reminds you that you are all friends, joining together to create.

TELEPHONE

Remember that old game where one person whispers to another and that person to another and so on? By the time the message reaches the last person, its meaning has completely changed. This is a written variation:

1,)   The first person will write down one line of dialogue.
2.)   The next will change it, tweak it, adding or subtracting a word or two.
3.)   The next will do the same and on and on until the entire group has had a shot.
4.)   The last person will then write a new line of dialogue in response to the final version of the previous line.
5.)   The next will change it.
6.)   The next will do the same and on and on.

Do this entire process for ten lines of dialogue.

                                                              15 minutes.

Read.

SEX AND MURDER

1.)   As a group decide on two character names you particularly like.
            Harry and Josephine.
2.)   Each person will write a scene where Harry is trying to get Josephine into bed. Josephine is trying to kill Harry.
         By the end of the scene, one has succeeded.

                                                              15 minutes.
3.)   Each person should circle 15 lines that he/she particularly likes.
4.)   Now, pair up into groups of two.
5.)   Using only the 30 lines between you, rewrite the "Harry and Josephine" scene. Feel free to add stage directions as necessary.

                                                              15 minutes.
Read.

LIFEBOAT

1.)   As a group, choose a scenario requiring escape.
            A stuck elevator whose cables won't hold.
            A small raft on stormy seas.
            A burning office building with sealed windows.

55.

power dynamics

structure

2.)   However many of you are in the group is the same number as those who are stuck in your scene. Each group participant will write the dialogue for their particular character.
All characters are stuck.
All want to escape.
All have different ideas about how to do it.
All believe that they are right.
All want to be heard.
All want to survive.

3.)   Elect your fastest typist to write this scene out.
4.)   Begin with a stage direction, "ALL are stuck in _____."
5.)   Go once around the circle, each person throwing out a line from their character's perspective.
6.)   Go once around the opposite way, doing the same.
7.)   Now go every other person.
8.)   Now every person who was skipped.
9.)   Every third person.
10.)   The first and last person.
11.)   The two people smack in the middle.
12.)   All say a line at the same time. (Do your best, typist!)
ALL YELL.
ALL CRY.
ALL LAUGH.
13.)   Go once around the circle.
14.)   Go once around the other way.
15.)   Write one last stage direction, "All escape." Or "All die."

Read.

40 minutes.

power dynamics

structure

56.

BE HERE NOW

Where am I? I have, at this point, written a whole lot.
I'm excited because I have pages and pages.
I'm scared because I have no idea what it all means.
I'm frustrated because I don't know if all this work is even leading to the creation of a play.

I do know that there are characters I sure like.
I do know that there are situations packed with drama that carry the story.
I do know that there are moments I want to find out more about.
I do know that I can choose these people, these scenes and these moments as the basis for my further explorations.

I am here, open.

THE MIDDLE

Middle: n.; The place in the thick of it.

ON CLARITY

We now have a collection of scenes, monologues, bits and pieces which are inspiring, depressing, boring, thrilling and fun.

This is the time to focus in.
Who excites you (the research may have helped you there!) and who holds no future?

This doesn't mean we cut off possibility. It means that our questions are posed to a select group, because, if we trust these specific characters and their needs, we will get our answers.

Now that we are deep into our process, trusting our exercises more than ever before, there are no longer set time constraints for our explorations. It is up to us to find out when the tale is told.

THE LETTER

If you don't know how to proceed or where exactly you are heading, this is good news. It means you are open to what the story is trying desperately to tell you.

1.)   Write a letter to yourself where you talk about your feelings about the piece.

       Let it all out.

       The anger, the frustration, the joy.

       Tell yourself why you started writing it (or writing anything at all) in the first place.

> *Aaron, you believe that people are flawed and that is WHY they are beautiful. Your lead character is a quintessential reminder of this and the more he tries to be perfect, the more alienated he becomes from his humanity. Don't forget that. It's important, it needs to be said, again and again!*

2.)   Circle 10 sentences from your letter.
3.)   Craft at least 3 scenes (refer to any of the exercises if you get stuck!) that must include all of those lines in some way, shape or form.

(side margin: plot development)

THE MONOLOGUE

Write a monologue where you are telling someone about your play. He just isn't getting it—not understanding the plot or the reason for its existence.

You must try every explanation and every tactic possible to get the other to hear, to see, to understand.

Be brutal, be difficult, be angry, be vulnerable.

This may take 10 minutes or it may take hours.
I encourage you to keep going forward as you work out the details, as you unpack the tale of the play.

Give yourself permission to let the story and its reasons for existing evolve.

plot development

THE CONVERSATION

A scene.

Set the stage.

Character A is you.
Character B is your protagonist.
You disagree about the play's story and how to tell it.

Fight, scream, yell, fuck.
Anything you need to do to get on the same page.
Just remember...you must have conflict!

Talk it out.
Become friends.
Find your way together.

plot development

PROLOGUE

That which comes before.

In my play, *A Terrific Tale of Ancient Terror!*, the protagonist sexually abuses his daughter throughout the course of the piece. In the prologue, however, we watch as he shields his daughter from a blazing fire with his body.

Traditionally, prologues are thought of as scenes or moments which demonstrate events prior to the main action of the play.

This can be true. I have found, however, that my prologues must accomplish one thing:

> *Allow the audience to see the play's intention.*

In *Terrific Tale...* that prologue scene stayed with the audience so that no matter what heinous acts the father performed, he was viewed as a man with protective instincts.

1.) In one or two sentences, write down what you, the author, want your audience to take away from the play.

> *I want the audience to feel empathy for Papa and for all "villains."*

2.) Your prologue scene must have the following elements.
One piece of factual information which must be imparted:

> *They live in a small house.*

One extreme action. Don't write, *he goes to the bathroom.* Instead write:

> *He shits out the entire world.*

Two characters. One must already exist in the world of the play. The other must not have appeared in your writing yet. Perhaps this is somebody from your character's past.

3.) Using the guidelines above, write your prologue scene as a fulfillment of "what you want your audience to take away from the play." Help them to see the play through your eyes.

structure

65.

THE LAST SCENE

Write the last scene of your play.
Find out how it all comes together.
How it all falls apart.
How it ends.

Write the scenes that lead us inevitably to this conclusion.

Do this again and again throughout your playwriting process.

The ending will probably shift and change.
This simply means that the play is revealing itself over time.

plot development

structure

THE LAST LAST SCENE

The ending of every old story is simply the beginning of a new one.

Write the scene immediately following the concluding moments.

Find out how life goes on.

plot development

structure

COLLAGE

How do we use our research, coupled with a growing awareness of where the play is headed, and apply it to the continuing development of your work?

Let's say you have found some wonderful quotes or a fantastic passage from a primary source. Here are some exercises for using these quotes effectively.

THE LONG FORM

1.)   Look for a continual two to three page passage. This can be a bible story, a famous speech, a spoken word poem—anything that relates to your play, either directly (such as a speech by your protagonist) or indirectly (such as a story from the Koran whose themes resonate in some way).

2.)   Type this speech out, word for word. Either your lead character or another character will say this entire passage.

3.)   Just above this passage, set the scene in no more than three lines:

> *An office on the thirty-fifth floor. Filthy and crowded.*
> *Our protagonist stands amidst the rubble.*

4.)   Now, every ten or so lines, leave a space on your page where you may insert stage directions.

5.)   After this has been completed, write ten lines of stage directions describing an action your character is engaged in while in this space. Allow the content and difficulty of this sequence to grow.

> *Odysseus picks up a piece of paper.*
> *Tosses it in the air.*
> *Picks up another piece.*
> *Rips it in two.*
> *Picks up a pile of papers.*
> *Shoves them down his pants.*

And onward.

Make sure your last stage direction hits a final high or low note.

> *Odysseus eats the rest of the papers, pushing them down*
> *every bodily orifice. He collapses.*

6.)   Now, go back into the main sequence and insert these stage directions in the empty spaces.

7.)   Reread and see what you have.

If you want to take this exercise further, feel free to rewrite the scene, replacing all quotes with new dialogue, which carries the same content (emotional and otherwise), but feels more organic to the figures you now know so intimately.

THE SHORT FORM (QUOTES, QUOTES, QUOTES)

1.) Write down seven to ten quotes from your research materials. They may carry great meaning or they might just be random points of interest.

2.) Next, give yourself a basic premise, depending on the needs of the developing story:

> *Your two characters are breaking up. One wants it to work, the other doesn't. One is actively trying to hide something from the other.*
>
> *Three supporting figures are conspiring to commit a murder and have different ideas about how it should be done.*

3.) In this scene, all chosen quotes must be said at least once.
The only restriction is that no character should present it as a quote. In other words, the lines should always grow directly from need and not as a comment on the interaction.

4.) Read the scene. You will probably find that people express themselves in bolder ways than you might have written otherwise.

5.) Again, rewrite if desired, using language which carries the same emotional weight.

plot development

making connections

69.

character creation

plot development

structure

AND GOD TALKS BACK

Why am I writing this?
Why is this journey so important?
Why is my main character on what seems to be a neverending search?
Why?
Why?
Why?

This monologue exercise was inspired by a student's work with Jesus in her play (the whole Holy Trinity shows up at the lead character's dinner table). She was stuck, unsure of what role he really played in the story. She had reams of material, as you probably now do, and felt paralyzed, afraid that the play was, after much hard work, to be abandoned.

It became apparent to us that she needed to allow him his pain, his disappointment and, above all, his desire. Of course, all of these things had to relate to the lead character and her place in life. As a result of doing the following work, the writer learned a great deal about her Jesus figure and, even more importantly, learned some fundamental things about her protagonist.

1.)   GOD, whatever that would be to your protagonist—Jesus, Buddha, Krishna, a biker chick, Charlton Heston, a talking frog—appears and speaks to your protagonist. This protagonist cannot hear God; she just goes about her business.

2.)   God reveals its wishes for your protagonist. God gets angry, yells, screams, punches—does whatever she has to do to be heard. God tells your protagonist her purpose on this Earth and even tells her what she must do to fulfill this purpose. Nothing works. God is not heard.

Now, this alone will tell you a great deal, but you can push it even further into full identification with the God figure.

3.)   After exhausting all options, God gets vulnerable. Speaks of the pain when he/she is not listened to. Feelings of rejection abound. Maybe God gives up, maybe God leaves or maybe God makes one last attempt to be heard by trying something new: whispering, crying, falling silent.

Read it. Take it in. Who is your figure and what is she avoiding? What would it take for her to listen to God or to anyone else, for that matter?

AND IT WAS GOOD

Write a separate scene where your character completely fulfills God's wishes for her.

Maybe she hears God.
Maybe she doesn't.
She does, however, find that divine freedom.
Revel in it.

character creation

OPPOSING WORDS

By this point in the process, I know my characters very well.
I have seen them begin.
I have seen them end.
Their ins and outs are no longer a mystery to me.
This is where my writing can become stagnant, devoid of spontaneity.

Before I continue, I must challenge myself to allow this channeled world to become as big as life. After all, there are very few things I would "never" say.

Give your characters the same freedom to live as fully as I hope we may give ourselves.

Use the figure who seems to be driving the story for this experiment.

1.)   Make a list of ten words you believe your character would never use.
2.)   Make a list of ten words your character uses fairly regularly.
3.)   Write a monologue where your character attempts to escape from Character B's violent clutches. Use all of the first set of ten words.
4.)   Use none of the second set.
5.)   Take it in.

When your character is pushed against the wall, how does he behave?
Is he: more vulnerable, softer, more eloquent, more profane?

WORDS OF COMFORT

Allow your character the permission to completely change gears with nary a moment's notice.

6.)   Continue the monologue right from where you left off. This is probably in the midst of struggle. Nothing has worked. The dilemma remains unresolved.
7.)   Give your character the permission to use the ten familiar words.
        She says them in no more than five sentences.
        At the end, Character B either gives in...or holds on tighter.

Read it again. How did it change? Did your character resort to familiar tactics or did she finally tell the truth? Why did this work? Why did it not?

Do this exercise with as many figures as you desire.
Let them speak without censorship.

DON'T GO THERE

What situation would your character avoid at all costs?
Where would he never go?
Who would she never be with?

Place her in that situation.
She is there.
She will do everything she can to escape.
To deny reality.
To fight.
Somehow, along the way, she comes to celebrate this predicament, finding the joy in this unexpected place.

If you want to warm up first, do this exercise with a family member as your lead character. Place your father with a heart condition on a high speed roller coaster. See how he fights and how he thrives.

ON MOTIFS

Look back through all that you have done.

A day
of reflection.
Make a list of images and moments that you dig.
That carry meaning.
That stick in the craw.

Keep this list handy.

As you continue writing, find ways to let these images repeat:

> *Boy, I liked the mirror image that came up while doing the Dream A Little Dream exercise. I will start this day's writing with that same mirror.*

When we start looking at your draft, the task of creating a satisfying alliance of symbols and themes will have already begun.

REWRITING *YOUR* MYTH

In my classes this is alternately known as Don't Fuck With My Myth, because even in its nascent stages, we become attached to what we've written and the great meanings which resonate from these writings.

You have discovered some possible endings for your play.
Find a new way to end this developing piece by utilizing the Rewriting the Myth exercise from the first section. Do the same steps with your own work.

30 minutes

After you are done, read it. This might be close to the truth, or it could be a bunch of bunk.

Either way, you are exploring your story's exciting possibilities.

character creation

plot development

making connections

GRIEF NEVER DIES

This is yet another way to use classic models of grief recovery to illuminate your play.

NUMBNESS

Like depression, this state is often described as an absence of feeling.
How can I write a negative? I can't.
I do this instead:

1.) Character A is performing some mundane action with a familiar object or piece of equipment.
Again and again and again without variation.
This should go on for at least half a page.

2.) Suddenly, the character realizes that he feels nothing. He stops.
Then tries it a different way.
A different way.
A different way.
A million different ways, attempting to regain sensation.
Nothing quite works.

3.) Finally the character throws whatever object he/she is working with to the ground and attempts to destroy it.

DISORGANIZATION

1.) Character A grabs other objects in the space.
He destroys each object in its turn.
This goes on and on for pages.
Think of as many objects as you can—large and small *(irons, rods, cars, houses, etc)*.

2.) Find various methods of destruction *(shooting, stomping, hitting, crashing, tearing apart, etc)*.

3.) Finally, Character A is surrounded by piles of broken things.

REORGANIZATION

1.) Character A slowly starts to pick through the pieces.
Attempts to put them back together.
Some pieces fit.
Others don't.
Tries to glue them, smash them together, gently massage them, and so on.

2.) Finally, after a mixture of success and failure, Character A calls out for help!

76.

character creation

Cries out.
Screams out.
3.)   Character B enters and tries to help.
        B may insist that A stop and rest.
        B may hold A and comfort him.
        B may pick up the pieces and patiently show the way.
        A lets himself be helped OR pushes B away.

What actions are your characters willing to receive and which ones just cause them to shut down?

Notice these things.

Let them enter your play when the time is right.

structure

BREATHE

Stop.
Breathe.
Take a walk.
Let your mind empty out.
Talk to God.
Talk to yourself.
Talk to the wind and to the strangers who pass you on the street, on your hike or in your backyard.
Answers will come.
You will hear that you should change certain words.
That your main character is in love with pain and you have to write a scene where he has a conversation with a wound.
You will hear that the play has no hope and you desperately want some.
You will hear the the setting is smaller and therefore bigger than you imagined.
You will let go of lines you are holding on to.
You will give birth to lines that speak more truthfully.
You will laugh at things that are funny.
You will cry at things that are not.
You will allow yourself to dream.
To imagine.
To live in the world.
To live in your play.
You will be writing while you are doing everything else.
You will be writing while you are doing nothing.
You will be writing.
Stop.
Breathe.
Talk.
Listen.
Dream.
Write.
Write.
Write.

SYMPATHY FOR THE DEVIL

I have an easy time identifying with my protagonists, my heroes.
I am able to let them speak their needs and I have compassion for their foibles.

At this point in the process, we have probably come to feel that there are opposing forces in our play. There are people trying to stop our primary figures from achieving their goals.

Before I can walk forward in this story, I have to fully identify with all my characters—villains and heroes, gods and devils alike.

Remember that every person is the hero of her own story.

Who best represents the opposing force in your play?
Who embodies destruction?
Who is getting in your main character's way?
Who is getting in your way, stopping the play from continuing because you and your characters don't know how to deal with him?
Who?

MONOLOGUE 1

1.)   Write down this person's characteristics.
      Make a list of all the things you hate.
      Make a list of all neutral things.
      Now make a list of admirable things.
2.)   Write a monolgoue. This figure is speaking to his mother or father. He is in need and believes that this parent is the only one who can fulfill that need.

MONOLOGUE 2

1.)   Write down the characteristics of this person's natural enemy; this may be your play's protagonist.
      The things you admire.
      Neutral.
      And the things not so admirable.

The following does not need to be, and perhaps should not be, consciously connected to the scene above.

2.)   Write a monologue.
        She is refusing to give in.
        She is defending her position with all guns blazing.
        She may even inflict bodily or verbal harm.
        She is speaking to a child, scolding.

DIALOGUE

1.)   Pull ten lines from section 1.
        Pull ten lines from section 2.
2.)   Create a dialogue between these two characters.
        You may only use the twenty chosen lines.
        In whatever order you wish.
        You may divide up the lines or keep them intact.
        Single words are acceptable.
        Use every last syllable.

Read it.

It might be interesting to note who has the power in this scene and who you wind up identifying with more.

character creation

plot development

making connections

CLIMAXING

What is the climax of a play?

A climax occurs when the heat is turned up so high that a choice needs to be made, the choice that the entire play has been leading us to.

A climax occurs when everything that has been held back, contained or prevented for the entire piece takes over.

A climax occurs when nothing will ever be the same again.

A climax occurs when the music which has lagged, sped up, lulled, turned pizzicato and legato, reaches its crescendo.

A climax is what we, the audience members, are waiting for.

If you do not yet know where your story is headed, this will help guide you towards the realizations your characters need to have and even, perhaps, clarify how they got there.

1.)   Write the inciting incident for your scene in one line.

> *James punches Sarah.*
> or
> *Stan receives his HIV test result.*

2.)   What is the immediate result of this action? Write it in one line.
3.)   Skip two pages. How does the scene end? What is the culmination of all that came before? Write it in one line.
4.)   Fill in the middle.

plot development

structure

character creation

plot development

making connections

MAKE ME LAUGH

For those of you who find yourself writing "tragedies" and projects packed with loss or grief (as most good dramatic stories are), this may help you see the full humanity and scope of your project.

1.)   Place your main character on stage in a comedy club.
       This is her chance to make everyone laugh.
       Many good comedians use pain as the basis for their humor.
       I would encourage you to do the same.
2.)   Your character should tell her tragic, painful, bereft and meaningful story during this set. At every turn though, the goal is laughter!
       Your character wants the audience to enjoy themselves, to relate and most importantly to double over with guffaws at the wry observations and goofiness of it all.
3.)   Look for the punchlines and play to them.

Remember, many comics use prolonged set-ups to lead to an even more surprising pay-off. Feel free to do this. You can present the story in classic dramatic ways, as long as they're all in service of the joke.

AN EXTRA STEP

At a certain point, probably late in the monologue, the jokes are not succeeding. Or the big joke that's been building fails miserably. Your main character is bombing.

So, she pulls out all the stops, doing everything she can to get the laugh.
Each joke should top the one before it.

This could, and probably should, include the addition of physical humor:
        pratfalls, juggling, facial gesture, props, etc.
Whatever it takes.

Don't forget, The Big Finish!
How does the set end?
Does she leave the stage, dropping the microphone like a hot potato?
Does she break a chair, letting the shards fly into the audience?
Does she take a small bow and say, "Goodnight Peoria! You're the greatest!"

MAKE ME LAUGH AGAIN!

The most dramatic moment in your play.

The part that calls for pathos and probably tears.

The greatest loss, the most painful memory, the turning point that leads to tragedy or salvation.

This is now a comedy. Write it.

Do not change the content of the scene.
If a murder occurs, it still must take place.
If a marriage falls apart, it must end.

Where, in the scene, does your main character spin out of control?
In a drama, this might be shown with a bout of screaming and crying. In a comedy, it might be shown with a bout of screaming and crying.

So, what makes the difference?

In the comedy, the screaming and crying goes to the extreme, the edge of what those actions might look like, and then goes over that edge with all arms flailing.

In my play *Strut,* Essie, a gorgeous Rita Hayworth type, falls and breaks her neck. She winds up in a surgical halo, doomed to a life as an invalid. In the piece, however, her collapse is a pratfall packed sequence, where a cymbal crash accompanies her every fall.

I composed that sequence by giving myself a specific comedic world to play in and then wrote the scene as though it was completely of that genre.
If you are unsure of how to begin, you may do the same.

Some suggestions:
Three Stooges slapstick, Marx Brothers, Mel Brooks, bad 1980's sitcom...

Write the scene as though it is completely of that world.

PLAYING WITH MUSIC

What is the music of your piece?

Is it a blues number, hard and soulful all at once?
Is it bubble gum pop, with deep wells of regret expressed to a jaunty tune?

Listen to some of that music for a good half hour. Let it sink into your ears and your hidden mind.

Choose one song (with lyrics, this is important) that speaks to your play clearly.

Pick three of your favorite lines from that song.

Write the scene that feels to you most like that song.
All three lines must be spoken.

Do this exercise for at least two other scenes, using a new song for each one.
Find the music of your piece and let it play.

power dynamics

structure

84.

FOUND OBJECTS

Do the Space Visualization exercise with one of the play's familiar figures.
Add these questions:
What objects are in the room?
Are these objects heavy or light?
Soft and flexible or rigid and hard?
What memories do these objects hold for you?
How do you feel about these objects?

There should be at least three objects in the space that your character can relate to.

SCENE ONE

This may be quite short. We are merely setting up the situation and letting it roll.
Your character picks up an object—or, depending on the circumstances, the object falls
into his hands or is thrust there by another figure in the space.

> Feel free to set the scene with a few lines of stage direction:
>
> *Jane is in the kitchen.*
> *Thomas bends over the stove. He knocks the ANTIQUE SALT
> SHAKER off the counter.*
> *Jane catches it just before it hits the floor.*

SCENE ONE AND A HALF

Upon contact with the object, the scene shifts so that the character is completely en-
gaged in a memory.

1.)   This scene begins with the main character somehow relating to this object.

2.)   This scene is a celebration of some kind.

> *A wedding, a bar mitzvah, an anniversary party, a romantic
> night with a lover*

The scene should be filled with laughter, joy, smiles and/or passion. All of the
hallmarks of enjoyment. Let it get big!

> *Raucous laughter, naughty jokes, a wall of sound.*

3.)   Once this has been established thoroughly and reached its crescendo, something
changes the mood.

> *A character says something upsetting, someone suddenly has*

85.

plot development

a heart attack...

4.)   The celebration then splits apart.

> *Everyone exits, leaving the main character alone, or*
> *everyone goes to separate corners of the room, making hur-*
> *ried phone calls on their cells.*

SCENE TWO

Back in the original space.

No more than ten lines of dialogue between Character A and the other figure in the room. This should pick up exactly where the scene left off at the top, with an argument growing but not yet erupting:

> *Jane: You should be more careful.*
> *Thomas: I'm doing the best I can.*
> *Jane: Fine.*
> *Thomas: Fine.*

Then continue with action/dialogue that leads to another object:

> *Thomas returns to cooking.*
> *Jane searches the cupboard for a mug.*
> *She reaches in and grabs the one saying, "Barcelona."*

SCENE TWO AND A HALF

As soon as the character comes into contact with this object, she is once again fully immersed in a different memory.

In this scene, the object must come into play at some point (if even for just a moment), but you do not need to begin with it.

Character A is trying desperately to retrieve something that has been lost. She will do whatever it takes to get it back.

SCENE THREE

The character is throttled back to the present before the conflict/need is resolved or fulfilled.

Begin this scene with a question:

> *Can't you help me?*

The argument erupts and another object comes into play.

SCENE THREE AND A HALF

One more memory.

Your hero has just been roundly and irretrievably defeated. She either finds a way to carry on anew or collapses in resignation. This can be done briefly with all stage directions or a monologue or some combination thereof.

The object does not come into play until the end of the scene. Perhaps it appears on the ground or it is found or...

CONCLUSION

Back to the original scene.

Our protagonist either gives up the argument, leaves the space, wins or offers compromise. Find out and see what happens.

An extra step. Find a way to have all three objects come into play here :

> *Jane smashes all objects to the ground.*
>
> or
>
> *Jane offers all objects to Thomas, who uses them for the finishing touches on a dish.*

plot development

power dynamics

structure

character creation

FOUR MONOLOGUES, TWO SCENES AND SO MUCH MORE

I find this particularly helpful when I have written a ton and feel as though I ain't got nothin' left.

Ask yourself: are there any significant moments in my protagonist's story that I have yet to touch? The answer will inevitably be "yes," if we are being honest.

ONE MONOLOGUE

Once you have answered that question, you should write the story of that significant moment in monologue form from your protagonist's perspective.

Keep in mind, though, NEED!
Your character has a need to convince somebody else that his story is significant, is necessary, must be heard because he/she wants understanding.

> *Officer, I stuck the knife in her throat cause she wouldn't shut her yap.*

Every seven lines, make a dramatic shift in tactic and increase the need.

The character never gives up, the need remains unfulfilled.

power dynamics

TWO MONOLOGUES

Write the monologue of the character on the other side, the one receiving this story. He is trying to convince your protagonist that his own story is more important. Follow the same guidelines as above.

THREE MONOLOGUES

Choose a tangential character from your piece, one who has some bearing on the story but may not have yet appeared or spoken.

structure

This character will now, in monologue, be asking for something from your protagonist. Perhaps a little sex or just a little comfort. Follow the same guidelines as above.

FOUR MONOLOGUES

Your protagonist once again. This time your character starts from the place she ended her original monologue: at the height of tactics and need.

character creation

Every seven lines, this need will become less great, and the tactic smaller, until your character is in surrender and acceptance.

SCENE ONE

What is the scene you want to write?
If none come to mind, you can use the same "scene scenario" as you used for your monologues above.

Write it using only lines from any and all of the four monologues.
Use as few or as many as you like.
Stick the lines in a new character's mouth if need be.

SCENE TWO

Another unwritten scene.
Same guidelines as above. Use the lines you have not yet explored.
You will have some lines left over. Save them, they may come in handy at any point in your process.

This is a great tool for focusing on the basic human needs, putting your characters at the height of those needs and then crafting scenes from such a charged place.

Do this whenever you find a scene you wish to see that just can't seem to get written.

power dynamics

making connections

character creation

DREAM A BIGGER DREAM

Look at a scene you've already written, one where a character came into conflict with another figure and that conflict was left either unresolved or resolved in a way that left your character wanting.

This sequence will follow that scene.

Perhaps, as you near the time to put together a draft (yes!), any questions you still have, any conflicts left hanging, will get resolved in this dream.

1.)   Make a list of five lines from the scene mentioned above.
2.)   List two locations: the one where the conflict took place and one from the past.
3.)   List two characters: the supporting figure from the conflict scene and a charac-
       ter who your figure has not yet met—perhaps, a future child or enemy or friend.
4.)   Now write the dream scene:
       Both locations must be used.
       Both figures must appear.
       One moment of violence.
       One moment of blatant sexuality.
       AND (here's my favorite part) your main character gets what he wanted in the
       previous scene, here in the dream. In other words, if Character A wanted an
       apology that was not given, he gets the apology in his dream.

making connections

SAY SAY SAY

1.)   Write nine lines that you love:
        Three of which you wish someone would say to you.
        Three of which capture the essence of your play—the things the audience
        MUST hear.
        Three of which make you giggle.
2.)   Choose one line from each category.
3.)   Write a scene in which these three lines MUST be spoken.

Six lines remain.

What is the scene you have not written?
The one you have been avoiding?
The moment you wish would happen?
The brutal confrontation you don't want to face?
The vulnerability you resist?
The relief that won't come?

4.)   Write that scene.
        Use all six lines.

plot development

making connections

EPILOGUE

That which comes after.

In *Hamlet* there is an epilogue of sorts. Fortinbras, the opposing warlord, comes into the castle with its dead bodies flung about, and takes his seat as the new ruler. This character has only been spoken of, but has not appeared anywhere during the domestic drama we have witnessed earlier.

An epilogue may give factual information. Think of those post–film titles where we learn the fates of the main characters. Even these tidbits tend to accomplish one thing above all else: they present the audience with a new or wider perspective.

When Fortinbras enters, we see the bloody, lust–filled, domestic drama as a metaphor for war and the futility of political machinations. Suddenly, we are forced to view *Hamlet* as a global problem, as opposed to a local one.

1.)   In one or two sentences, write down what new light you want the audience to see at the end of your play.

> This may be posed in the form of a question:
> *If we cannot find peace at home, can we ever find it outside our walls?*

The elements:
One piece of factual information.
One extreme action.
One character must appear who has not appeared in your play or has appeared in a different form. For example, you may choose to follow Shakespeare's lead and include a character who has been spoken of but not realized, or you may include a future version of a character we have already met.

2.)   Write the scene with an eye on posing the new question to your audience.

structure

BE HERE NOW

Where am I?
I have a ton of writing.
More than I think I need.
Fragments.
Bits.
Pieces.
Dangling feet and flailing arms.
Words, Words, Words.

I may have gone back to write some of the exercises once again. I may have discovered new elements, new characters, new scenarios and followed them down rabbit holes. I may have revisited page one, page five, page twelve—again and again and again.

I am ready to discover my play.

I am here, on the verge.

THE END

End: n.; The outer boundary.

ON PUTTING IT TOGETHER

"The first draft of anything is shit."
                    —Ernest Hemingway

Ah, gotta love Ernie's optimistic thinking.

What he says is true, but it's only half the story.

Yes, the first draft is often simplistic, unfocused, over-written and thematically at sea (to borrow from Ernest once again). But it's also filled with ideas, raw emotion, uncensored streams of imagination and key plot elements.

Above all, it is necessary.

OPERATING METAPHOR

I don't outline. There, I said it.
I do, however, discover a shape.
A form.
A structure.

If my play is about a 1940's swing dancing couple, it flows like a Gershwin tune, light and jaunty in the beginning, with pockets of sadness towards the middle and a resolution that's bittersweet.

If my play is about a man saying goodbye to his wife who silently wastes away, it goes from ritual and repetition to fight, to exhausted surrender, to freedom.

If my play is about a flood and its victims, it starts with trickles of information, moves into an overwhelming storm of emotion and finally, resolves with a wiping away of all that has come before.

The play tells me what its shape should be.

As I dive into draft creation, my only job is to listen.

MIND THE GAP

This is the first of two draft construction exercises. Try both and then settle on the one which feels most interesting and organic to your play's needs.

Fire up the PC (or Mac, for those so inclined).

1.)   Start a new document.
        At the top, put "AT RISE."
        A lot of old plays have that phrase at the beginning because the performance would start in earnest when the velvety red curtain slowly rose.
        It lends a little flair to our whole enterprise.
2.)   Next, write an opening stage direction for your play.
3.)   Then go into the scenes/monologues you have already written.
        Choose one. This is the first scene of your play.
        Paste it into the document.
4.)   Choose the next logical bit and paste it.
        And on and on.
        Use EVERYTHING you have written.
        Jumble it up.
        Pull single words and lines and put them in unexpected places.
        ALL OF IT.
        Feel free to add stage directions where you see fit.
5.)   Now read what you have in one sitting.
6.)   Mark the places where there are gaps that must be filled.
        Number these gaps.
7.)   Make a list of scenes/monologues/bits that would fill these spaces.

> For example, one of my lists might look like this:
> 1.)   *Shaw dances on the grave.*
> 2.)   *Coltrin seduces Shaw.*
> 3.)   *They travel to the moon.*
> 4.)   *Shaw walks across town...*

You will probably have at least twenty of these.
8.)   Write the first five gap scenes and paste them into your draft.
9.)   Write the last five gap scenes and paste them into your draft.
10.)   Read what you have.
11.)   Now write the rest of the gap scenes. (Actually, what remains might be made up of moments, monologues, scenic changes...)
12.)   Paste them into your draft.

plot development

structure

10 MINUTE, 20 MINUTE, 30 MINUTE...DRAFT!

This method of rapid draft creation is more plot centered than the previous exercise and asks you to think about your story in more conscious ways.

10 MINUTE PLAY

Write a ten page version of your play.

This should include:

1.)   An inciting incident.
2.)   At least one scene where the protagonist is dealing with the consequences of the inciting incident.
3.)   A concluding scene/moment.

This should be all new material, even if you feel you have dealt with some of these moments already.

20 MINUTE PLAY

Next, write a twenty page version of your play.

Use the previous 10 minute version as your base.

1.)   Expand your opening scene, by incorporating elements from a previously written material, perhaps a prologue scene or additional dialogue in the beginning section.
2.)   Take at least one pre-written scene and find where it can go in your middle section—before or after the scene you just wrote. Feel free to tweak the scene as needed. Cut bits and write new bits if necessary.
3.)   If you have written any ending moments previously, incorporate one of them into your new ending or tack it onto the end as an epilogue.

30 MINUTE PLAY

1.)   Read over your 20 minute play. Look at your old material and see if there are any scenes you feel MUST be in your play.
2.)   Put 'em in there.
        This is where you may find that you have to write connections, between the old and the new. This exercise may take up to an hour to read and pull material, and another 2 hours to paste and incorporate the old material in a fluid manner.

plot development

structure

At the end of the 5 or so hours this whole process may take, you will have a 30 minute draft of your play and some sense of a through-line. You will also have a clear idea of what may be missing (some of which you have probably already written).

Go back and fill in the gaps.

Feel free to use this to create your draft.
Or the previous exercise.
Or some combination thereof.
It's your play and your choice.

plot development

structure

FILLING IT IN

The previous exercises in this section talk about "filling in" the missing pieces.

Sometimes, this will require writing a whole new scene.
Sometimes, a single stage direction will do.
And, once in a while, a dance or song can have its say.

Whatever the case may be, remember, we are human beings.
We are wired to create stories.
To solve problems.
To make meaning.

This won't always be fun.
It may even feel like work.
Well, it is.

And, as with any hard work, when our backs hurt and our fingers ache and our minds reel while our bodies sweat, we feel satisfied when the work is done.

CONGRATULATIONS

You have finished DRAFT ONE of your play.

Celebrate.
Have a good meal.
Have a drink.
Go see a movie.
Pat yourself on the back.

Enjoy today.

READ!!

A few years back, over the course of one summer, I read about one hundred and fifty plays. Do I remember the details of half of them? No. What I do recall, though, somewhere deep in my bones, are their structures, the things that made them compelling, alive, brimming with conflict—in a word, theatrical.

Before we head into the next part of our play's development, let's remember those who have come before us and who still have plenty to teach us.

Here's a partial list of must-reads.

Strindberg:
Dream Play
The Dance of Death: Parts I and II
Miss Julie

Ibsen:
Little Eyolf
Peer Gynt

Pinter:
Betrayal
Old Times
The Birthday Party

Beckett:
Endgame
Krapp's Last Tape
Act Without Words: I and II

O'Neill
Long Days Journey Into Night

Richard Foreman:
The Mind King

Suzan Lori Parks:
Topdog/Underdog

Genet:
The Maids

Lillian Hellman:
Toys in the Attic

Brecht:
The Resistible Rise of Arturo Ui
The Good Woman of Setzuan

Mac Wellman:
A Murder of Crows

Caryl Churchill:
Cloud Nine

Thornton Wilder:
The Skin of Our Teeth

Len Jenkin:
Dark Ride

Shakespeare:
The Tempest
Hamlet

Shepard:
Buried Child
Cowboy Mouth

Sophocles:
Antigone

Albee:
Seascape
Zoo Story

Matthew Maguire:
The Tower

Paula Vogel
How I Learned to Drive

Mary Zimmerman:
Metamorphoses

Texts or performance archives from The Living Theatre, The Open Theatre, The Wooster Group and Theatre de Complicite.

This is just a small selection and an eclectic mix particular to my own off-center tastes.

Happy Readings!

THIS IS CRITICAL

You're about to ask yourself some tough questions about your play and its existence. Here's a way to get ready for the task.

When you go to see a theatre piece, start asking yourself about what worked and why, and, just as importantly, what didn't and why not.

Now, I do recommend letting the piece marinate—be moved, cry, laugh, enjoy! Let those feelings sit. Bask in them, revel in appreciation. Take a day or two if you need it.

We are, after all, people who love the theatre!

Then, begin the investigation:
What did I like?
What moved me?
Who did I identify with?
What aspect of the story seemed to take center stage?
What bored me?
What left me feeling pandered to?
What opportunities were fully unpacked?
What opportunities were left unexplored?
How could the writer have gotten more curious and left me with a richer experience?
What elements were inherently theatrical and could only happen live, while I sit there watching?
What elements were extraneous?
What shorthands and shortcuts were used to tell the story and give me exposition?
Where was exposition unnecessary?
Where did the play trust the audience?
Where did the play leave out important information?
Did the staging match the tone and intention of the piece and did the production obscure or reveal the play's characters, needs, themes, story...?

BE HERE NOW

Where am I?
I have discovered.
I have been in it.
I have accomplished.
I have taken a breather.

I don't think I am ready to go back into the play.
I may never be ready.

But the play has only just found its story.
That story may need help to speak more effectively.
To communicate clearly.
To have rhythm.
To be what it knows it can be.

I am here, reluctantly.

THE BEGINNING

Begin: v.; To come into existence.

ON "REWRITING"

A lot of writers don't like this term. I understand why.
It indicates an attempt to fix that which is broken.

Nothing is broken.
Nothing needs fixing.

Everything is right in front of you, just waiting to be seen for what it already is.

This is what "rewriting" does.
It paints the picture which has been sketched out so beautifully.

THERE IS NO ONE WAY

There are as many plays, scenes, monologues as there are artists, dreamers, people.

What for you is essential and necessary is merely icing on the cake for another.

What for you is abhorrent is for another delectable.

What for you is "to die for" may be unspeakable to your dearest friend.

I don't know how to be all things to all people. So the only thing I can be is of service to the play.

This requires a high level of honesty. If I am really listening to the play, I may have to discard whole pages and write new ones. I may have to look at a monologue and keep only one line that speaks truth. I may have to ask where the main character's journey is ragged, deviating from his or her needs?

Once I've done the work, however, no one can give me THE ANSWER. No one else can tell me whether the job is done or the work is just beginning. No one can relieve me of my doubts about the storytelling or the humor or the humanity.

No one.

No one, but the play itself.

ATTENTION MUST BE PAID!

That is, of course, the famous line from Arthur Miller's seminal work, *Death of a Salesman.*

And I agree.
We must pay close attention to that which is important.
To that which tells the tale.
That which carries weight.
And that which is just the wind, making a lot of noise, and blowing only momentarily through the trees.

1.)   Choose a favorite play.
        One you KNOW.
        One you CHERISH.
        One you BELIEVE is perfect.
2.)   Choose 100 lines.
        These lines should be primarily dialogue.
        Important stage directions (Willie dies) may, however, be included.
        These lines should be culled from throughout the play as evenly as possible
        (If it's a five act, don't pull 50 lines from Act 1).
3.)   Write the play using only these 100 lines.
        Tell the story.
        Embody the characters.
        Be brutal.
        Be quick.
        Be creative.
        PAY ATTENTION!
4.)   Try it with your own play.

Read it.

Oh, that's the story!

rewriting

NO IFS, ANDS OR BUTS

1.)   Read over a scene.
        Make a few notes to yourself about what the characters want from each other and
        what the scene is telling you about their relationship. How do they feel about
        sharing space with each other? Read your notes.

2.)   Remove any extraneous pre–wordage. In other words, cut transitions such as

> *So, Well, Then, But, And, However, Than, Yes (as in Yes, I
> see), No (as in No, I don't think that's true)...*

        Now, reread the scene and see if this change forces your characters to make
        larger emotional and logical leaps.

3.)   Now that you can see how much larger the leaps can be, rewrite the scene
        completely, having your characters express the extreme (or subtext, if you will)
        of what they are already saying. Look back at your Step One notes, if this helps.
        For example:

> Original: *But you don't live here.*
> Step One: *You don't live here.*
> Step Two: *Get out, motherfucker!*

4.)   Go through your whole play in this manner.

        How much more alive is it?

THE NEW PLAY

One time, I had very quickly finished the first draft of a piece. I put together the piece in a slapdash, I-just-wanna-see-this-thing-done fashion.

I then spent the next three months attempting to tweak it, adjust it, shift this to here and that to there.
Nothing worked.

Finally, I got humble and surrendered what I had written.

I told myself I was starting a new play. One that just happened to share characters and situations with the old one.

Two months later, I had a new piece with a new lead character.
It was thirty pages shorter than the previous version and its themes and story were abundantly clear.

I feel lucky.
I now have two plays.
One is raw, exciting, quick and dirty.
And it is just for me.
Maybe moments from it will find themselves in other plays.
Maybe scenes will become short plays which will stand on their own.
Maybe I'll just know it's on the shelf and get some measure of satisfaction.

The other digs deep.
This one is for the world.

The body of work grows.

rewriting

MAGNIFICATION

Sometimes, I read a scene and can't quite put my finger on why it's not yet serving the play. I know, however, that there is something vital to the play's life in there, waiting for me to get curious about it.

1.)   Choose a moment from any scene.
        A single line.
        A single pause or silence.
        A single laugh.
        A single scream.
        A single fuck.
        A single accusation.
2.)   Skip three pages.
3.)   Write the next moment or line which occurs in the scene.
4.)   Fill in the middle.
        Use all the tools at your disposal.
        Tactic after tactic after tactic.

Hell, this could be a seven step play in and of itself.

Read it.

This is how full every moment of your play can be.
How much life exists in every frozen second.

Keep this scene if you like.
Put the whole thing in your play.
Or just a line from it.
Or none of it.

But now you know what lurks there underneath.

MAGNIFICATION 10X

Repeat the exercise with a section of the scene above.
And then with a section of that scene.
And the next.
And the next...

Breathe.

THIS ONE'S MY FAVORITE

We all have that one scene we've written—the one we are sure needs no rewrites, that speaks truth and tells us exactly what the play wants us to hear.

1.)   Look at that scene—quickly! Don't read it. Scan it.
        What is the gist, the basic rhythm, the conflict?
2.)   Now, start over.
        You may use the first line of the already written version to begin. From there, write the scene again. You may find that you are using some of the same lines and moments. That's fine!

Do this for twenty to thirty minutes, challenging yourself to never look at the original version during the time.

At the end, see what you have.
How is it different?
What new tactics do your characters try out?
What new reasons are presented?
What new feelings result?

Throw this scene out.
Or keep it.
Or combine it with the original, revealing new truths.

rewriting

THEY ARE ALL MY FAVORITES

Do the previous page's exercise with your entire play.

Look over the play.
Get just a sense of it.

Now rewrite the entire thing.
You may find some moments fall away, while new ones pop up.
You may find some lines are needed and others you've forgotten ever existed.

You may find your play.

rewriting

ON KNOWING

You have, by now, written hundreds of pages.
You have written a play.
You have written a new play.
You have taken a chunk from there.
A slice from here.
And a whole lot from...

You can do each of these exercises a thousand times.
You can do them once.
You can go back through the play again and again.
Until it is truer.
Until it is stronger.
Until it is weaker.
Until it is...

You know worlds about story structure.
You know galaxies about people.
You know universes about this, all of it, tossed out pieces of paper, fragments of thoughts and split sentences and...

You know your play.

Trust yourself.

Write it.

BE HERE NOW

Where am I?
I am tired.
I am exhilarated.
I am ready to hear this thing spoken aloud.

I am here, anxious.

THE MIDDLE

Middle: n.; Intermediate of some basis of reckoning.

ON WAITING

When I first started writing, I was so excited to have a "finished" product that I would rush out, send the script to folks, open myself to feedback and wait for the responses to roll in.

Patience.
Silence.
Stillness.
I now recommend these highly.

It it truly wonderful that you have a written work.

It is also truly wonderful to sit and wait.

In a week or a month, go back and look at the work.

See if new questions arise.

Use all the exercises and tools now at your disposal to find answers.

GIVING IT AWAY

Ask yourself:

> *What does the piece need and am I (and is the play itself)*
> *ready to get outside feedback towards solving that need?*

If yes: give the work to only those you trust.

You may trust your wife.
Your husband.
Your best friend.
Your barber.

But whose insights do you trust?
Who do you believe will take the work at face value?
Who do you feel can put their own ego aside and be of service?
Who will be honest?

Then, ask that person(s) the big questions:

> *Is this character's need clear here?*
>
> *Did you understand the details of their relationship?*
>
> *Was the connection between these moments effective?*

Without providing this structure, you may get responses that, while valuable, are simply opinions.

Breathe.

One more time.

READINGS AND STAGED READINGS AND WORKSHOPS...OH MY!

I often find myself returning to the piece again and again.
Shifting single words.
Changing moments.
Or collapsing whole scenes.
However I do it, the work continues.

I do not believe every piece needs to go through years of changes, of readings, work-shops and feedback sessions.

Spare me the torture!

I do, however, think that these scenarios can be of great value if you are clear on WHY.

> Reasons to do readings and workshops:
> *To hear the play.*
> *To experience audience reaction.*
> *To work on the play throughout the process.*
> *To learn about the play.*

READINGS

A reading can happen anywhere.
In a theater.
A living room.
An empty space.
Around a table.
It can be cold (no rehearsal).
It can be warm (1–3 rehearsals).
It will usually have no staging.

What a reading can accomplish:
Let me hear my play.
Let me feel where it sings and where it sinks.
Expose new possibilities in the work.
Expose places which are still unfinished.
Expose places that can be cut.
Expose that which is easily accessible.
Reveal that which requires time and care to understand.

What a reading cannot accomplish:
Give a full theatrical experience.
Explore every possibility for every line and scene.
Have fully realized performances.
Replace actual production.

STAGED READINGS

I used to be averse to these scenarios.
I did not believe that they served the play or the playwright.
Imagine trying to do a love scene with script in hand. Yikes.
As my own work has grown, however, I have learned that staged readings can be effective if used purposefully.

When a piece has a large visual component or relies heavily on movement to tell its tale, just hearing the words can limit the playwright's understanding of her own work. Limited movement, a well timed turn of the head or a placement of Character A over here and Character B over there can create a partial visual picture, allowing the writer a glimpse into what she has created.

If you go this route, a highly experienced director whose first objective is to serve the play, as opposed to showcasing his directing chops, is imperative.

WORKSHOPS

A workshop production is often fully staged, with minimal tech and no script in hand. This is an opportunity for us to really work on the play, with a sense of how it moves, flows and where it breaks down. All involved, if we are lucky, know it is about developing the play, not about the production itself.

So, after every rehearsal, go home, change things, move them from here to there.
See how the changes play the next day.
And again the next day.
And the day after that...

THESE ARE NOT PRODUCTIONS. THEY ARE OPPORTUNITIES TO WORK ON THE PLAY!

Begin.

BE HERE NOW

Where am I?
I have written.
I have rewritten.
I have exposed the play to friends, to colleagues, maybe even to the invited public.
Maybe I have written some more.

I am wanting more.
Plays are not novels. They are of the theatre and are meant to be performed.
I do not know how "more" will happen.

I am scared this piece will never live out its purpose.
I am excited this piece may get to live out its purpose.

I am here, ready.

THE END

End: n.; A joining.

OUT IN THE WORLD

Theatre: (n.) A place of action; a field of operations.

We write plays to see them on their feet, big and bold, living out loud for many, not just ourselves, to experience.

There are as many ways to have a piece produced as there are plays.

We may go into the center of the street, proclaiming our words to the masses.

We may gather our troops in an abandoned warehouse and perform in secret by candle-light for anyone who may stumble upon us.

We may rent a space, print some postcards and invite our friends.

We may send packet after packet to theatre company after theatre company, hoping for a bite.

We may get to know a group of folks we admire, whom we can learn from, who are open and free, and invite them into our process.

We may write another play while this one waits in the wings.

We may build community.

Above all, remember:
We are not our work.
We are not our plays.

We put it out in the world and must let go of the outcome.

WHO DO YOU LIKE?

Your work has inherent value.
Anyone would be privileged to produce it.

It's up to you to decide whom you would like to offer this gift to.

When you go to see a piece of theatre, look at the program.

Ask these questions:

> *Is this a theatre company I'd like to work with?*
> *Who is the artistic director?*
> *Who is the literary manager?*
> *Who are the affiliated artists?*
> *How often does this company produce?*
> *What is the mission?*
> *If I want to get involved, how can I?*

Start establishing relationships.
Say hello. Theatre folk are friendly.

See where it goes from there.

134.

SUBMISSION

If you submit your work to theaters you do not know personally:
Find out which has a mission that intrigues you.
Talk to friends.
Read theatre sections in newspapers from around the country.
Every time a theatre company's name comes up, write it down and look it up.
See touring shows produced by exciting groups.
Find out whom your inspirations (favorite writers and artists, often quite established) are working with.
Look up whom your contemporaries (other writers who thrill you) are working with.
Take risks.

Some theatres accept unsolicited submissions.
Some do not.
Some require a fee to read your script. (I tend to stay away from those as I feel my work is of inherent value.)
Some do not.
Some accept email submissions.
Some require hard copies.
Some will respond to your submission, no matter the outcome.
Some will not.

RESOURCES

A selection of resources for finding theatres and, often, their guidelines for submission.

1.) *www.playwritingopportunities.com* — A clearinghouse for virtually every call for submissions in the United States.
2.) *www.enavantplaywrights.yuku.com* — Similar, but with a larger focus on short work.
3.) *www.pwcenter.org* — The Playwrights' Center in Minneapolis. A professional organization which lists some wonderful opportunities.
4.) *www.doollee.com* — An online attempt to list every play in the English language. It also includes a comprehensive listing of theatre companies throughout the world.
5.) *American Theatre Magazine* — A periodical focusing on what is happening throughout the country, with a fair amount of topical articles with "top theater makers." In the back is a listing of a theaters and their season offerings.
6.) *The Dramatists Sourcebook* — Considered "The Bible" of U.S. play submissions, contests and fellowship opportunities.

ON HUMILITY

When I enter a play production process, I try to remember:

I am collaborating.

I am working with other artists.

I have written for the live theatre, where almost everything is out of my control.

I do not know every meaning of every moment in the play.

I do not know the only way the set can look.

I do not know the best and only way to say a line.

I do not need everyone to "get it" from day one.

I do not need every second to be what I had imagined.

I do need to be inquisitive.

I do need to help the director understand the piece.

I do need to trust those I am working with.

ON CONFIDENCE

I try not to forget:

I do have a say, if I want it, in who gets cast.

I do have a right to expect the words to be said as written.

I do have a right to my opinion.

I do have a right to make requests on behalf of the play's needs.

I can say no.

I can say yes.

I can say, "Give it a try."

I can say, "I'll get back to you on that."

I can say, "I changed my mind."

I am the play's biggest advocate.

I fight for the play.

I surrender to the play.

BE HERE NOW

Where am I?

Here.
Most definitely.

THE BEGINNING

ACKNOWLEDGEMENTS

Thank you.

The Robey Theatre Company and the Playwrights' Program, for being a wonderful place to share much of this curriculum.

Son of Semele Ensemble, where I have grown as a person and as a writer.

Wordspace, Writing Pad, and great teaching partnerships.

Ben Guillory. For guidance and spirited discussions.

Edgar Landa. Your artistic eye and good humor.

Leon Martell, my first playwriting teacher. Enough said.

Brenda Varda. Your creative spirit. (And for looking over this damn thing!)

Chiwan and Judy. Your insight.

Al Watt. Friendship and inspiration.

The King Cat Crew (Laura, Michael and Mark). You know why.

Jamie and Alec. Through all the times...

Lisa and Chet. Wine and Theatre. God bless us, everyone!

The Guys and Friday Nights.

Sam and Renee. For caring.

Marty and Leslie. For sharing.

Julie. For being my teacher and partner.

And last, but not least, my students who allowed me to test these techniques with them.

Thank you for trusting me with you words, your minds, your hearts, and above all else, your truths.

Aaron Henne's plays include *King Cat Calico Finally Flies Free!* (published by Original Works Publishing), *Record Storm Spreads Ruin!* (commissioned by the Los Angeles History Project) and *Sliding Into Hades*, which received LA Weekly Awards for Playwriting and Production of the Year. Aaron has served in script development capacities for Culture Clash, The Colony Theatre, Center Theatre Group and The Theatre @ Boston Court, where he serves as Co-Literary Manager. Mr. Henne also works with spoken word and movement based techniques. His exploration of machines and their relationship to humanity, *Body Mecanique*, was developed and produced by LA Contemporary Dance Company. He teaches writing for the Playwrights' Program at The Robey Theatre Company, Writing Pad and runs the writer's studio, Wordstrut. Aaron is a proud member of The Playwrights Union.

CPSIA information can be obtained at www.ICGtesting.com
Printed in the USA
BVOW051323250613

324261BV00004B/6/P